THE LITURGIES OF QUAKERISM

The Liturgies of Quakerism explores the nature of liturgy within a form of worship based in silence. Tracing the original seventeenth century Quakers' understanding of the 'liturgy of silence', and what for them replaced the outward forms used in other parts of Christianity, this book explains how early Quaker understandings of 'time', 'history', and 'apocalyptic' led to an inward liturgical form.

The practices and understanding of twenty-first century Liberal Quakers are explored, showing that these contemporary Quakers maintain the same kind of liturgical form as their ancestors and yet understand it in a very different way. Breaking new ground in the study of Quaker liturgy, this book contrasts the two periods and looks at some of the consequences for the study of liturgy in general, and Quakerism in particular. It also explores evangelical Quaker understandings of liturgy.

'Ben' Pink Dandelion works as Programmes Leader, Centre for Postgraduate Quaker Studies Woodbrooke Quaker Study Centre in association with the University of Birmingham. He is editor of *Quaker Studies* and Convenor of the Quaker Studies Research Association. He is Series Editor for the Edwin Mellen series in Quaker Studies. His previous work includes *A Sociological Analysis of the Theology of Quakers: the silent revolution* (Mellen, 1996) and editor of *The Creation of Quaker Theory: insider perspectives* (Ashgate, 2004). He is co-editor of *The Historical Dictionary of the Friends (Quakers)* (Scarecrow, 2003) and co-author of *Towards Tragedy/Reclaiming Hope* (Ashgate, 2004).

D1546490

LITURGY, WORSHIP AND SOCIETY

SERIES EDITORS

Dave Leal, Brasenose College, Oxford, UK
Bryan Spinks, Yale Divinity School, USA
Paul Bradshaw, University of Notre Dame, UK and USA
Gregory W. Woolfenden, Ripon College, Cuddesdon, Oxford, UK
Phillip Tovey, Diocese of Oxford and Oxford Brookes University, UK

This new series comes at a time of great change in liturgy and much debate concerning traditional and new forms of worship, the suitability and use of places of worship, and wider issues concerning the interaction of liturgy, worship and contemporary society. Offering a thorough grounding in the historical and theological foundations of liturgy, books in the series explore and challenge many key issues of worship and liturgical theology which are currently in hot debate – issues set to make a significant impact on the place of the church in contemporary society. Presenting an ecumenical range of books, comparing and contrasting liturgical practices and concerns within various traditions and faiths, this series will appeal to those in university and theological colleges; adult education colleges; those on other ministry or lay ministry training courses; and practitioners and those involved in worship in churches across a broad ecumenical range.

Other titles in the series include

Death Liturgy and Ritual
Volume I: A Pastoral and Liturgical Theology
Volume II: A Commentary on Liturgical Texts
Paul P.J. Sheppy

Daily Liturgical Prayer
Origins and Theology
Gregory W. Woolfenden

Rituals and Theologies of Christian Baptism
Beyond the Jordan
Bryan D. Spinks

Inculturation of Christian Worship
Exploring the Eucharist
Phillip Tovey

The Liturgies of Quakerism

PINK DANDELION
Woodbrooke Quaker Study Centre
in association with the University of Birmingham, UK

ASHGATE

Published by
Ashgate Publishing Limited
Gower House
Croft Road
Aldershot
Hampshire GU11 3HR
England

Ashgate Publishing Company
Suite 420
101 Cherry Street
Burlington, VT 05401-4405
USA

Ashgate website: http://www.ashgate.com

British Library Cataloguing in Publication Data
Dandelion, Pink
    The liturgies of Quakerism. – (Liturgy, worship and society)
    1.Society of Friends – Liturgy
    I.Title
    264.'096

Library of Congress Cataloging-in-Publication Data
Dandelion, Pink.
    The liturgies of Quakerism/Pink Dandelion.
        p. cm. -- (Liturgy, worship and society series) Includes bibliographical references and index.
    ISBN 0-7546-3128-1 (alk. paper) -- ISBN 0-7546-3129-X (pbk. : alk. paper)
    1. Society of Friends--Liturgy. 2. Society of Friends--Doctrines. 3. Meditation--Society of Friends.
4. Public worship--Society of Friends. I. Title. II Series.

BX7737.D36 2004
264'.096--dc22   2003024251

ISBN 0 7546 3128 1 (Hbk)
ISBN 0 7546 3129 X (Pbk)

Printed on acid-free paper

Typeset by Tradespools, Frome, Somerset
Printed and bound in Great Britain by Antony Rowe Ltd, Chippenham, Wilts

Contents

List of Figures

Foreword

This foreword is offered by an Anglo-Catholic who has written frequently about his own liturgy and now, upon reading *The Liturgies of Quakerism*, has had to adjust his understanding of what the word 'liturgy' means.

Sociologists often make a distinction between latent and manifest functions. A manifest function is the purpose which an action or institution purports to serve; a latent function is its effect in the event. So universities have the manifest function of providing higher education and the latent functions of introduction bureaux for young people seeking partners.

Within the Christian faith, much of the action that takes place during the time identified as worship may be analysed in this way. The Anglican preacher may preface the sermon with such words as 'In the name of the Father and of the Son and of the Holy Spirit'. In those words the thoughts that follow are given a kind of authority. Then the people sit down. The words function thereby as a cue. Sometimes the preacher will announce the stage directions by saying, for example, 'Will you be seated?' At other times and in other places the preacher uses a more prolix prayer: 'May the words of my lips and the thoughts and meditations of all our hearts be now and always acceptable in thy sight, O Lord our strength and our Redeemer.'

For those who are sensitive about traditions of churchmanship, this is less of a Catholic acclamation. It may therefore be calculated to convey a message from a preacher to a congregation about mutual affiliation to the more protestant end of the Church of England. I am a preacher myself and I sometimes use the longer prayer for yet another reason: on a cold day or in a strange church, it gives an extended opportunity to test the acoustics and adjust my voice while the people are settling down. But I would not use the typical form of the Gospel Standard Strict and Particular Baptists; even though I might own the basic sentiment I would not express it in terms as unfamiliar to my audience: 'If the Lord should help me, I would direct your hearts to that solemn word in the book of Job.'

There are many other examples of dual or triple function in Anglican liturgy. The priest regularly bows to assistants in the act of worship. If the priest bows to the verger upon being escorted to the lectern or pulpit, it is not a gesture of subservience but of dismissal; the same is true when the priest places the offertory on the altar and turns to bow to those who have borne it thither. A nudge or a wink would serve the same purpose but thankfully do not yet belong in the vocabulary of Anglican ritual. Yet again, the celebrant first makes private communion then invites the people to come forward to make their own by facing them and using a form of words such as 'The things of God for the people of God': the function of these words as a theological statement is otiose but their usefulness in the choreography of the liturgy is paramount.

And so it is in the Quaker meeting. When the Elder observes 'Our Friend has given us much to ponder', the primary intention is not to appreciate the richness of the ministry. It cannot be that, for there is no significant tradition of complimenting ministers when they sit down. Its manifest function is not that which a stranger may suppose. Rather, it is a mechanism of control: the intention is to plead for a prolonged silence before the next ministry and those who speak the language of Quaker worship will take the hint.

Those of us who believed that liturgy was a matter of text in the narrow sense must open our minds to a more inclusive understanding. We are reminded in Dr Dandelion's Introduction that liturgy is about *work*, not about script: it is about the means made available for getting worship done. That such means are not voiced does not mean that they are not known. Whereas in the Anglican tradition the regulation of behaviour has tended to be inserted in the text as stage directions called 'rubrics', the unprogrammed Quaker tradition deploys a book of order; the Elders know the rules and members recognize the conventions for implementing them. For example, they learn to be inconspicuously vigilant for the handshake that signals the end of the meeting and the disintegration of silence.

Of course, there is more to liturgy than stage management. It has to do with the definition and transmission of agreed meanings. In the Church of England there exists a Liturgical Commission which presided over the changing of the form of addressing God from *thou* to *you* and adjusting the script of the people's greeting 'with thy spirit' to 'also with you'. The Commission has a constitutional authority if not an absolute influence. Whether they are set down on a page and given to the faithful to recite or are learnt as part of a group vocabulary, words matter. *Lex orandi, lex credendi*. The very word 'Friend' conveys the sense of a non-hierarchical and accepting relationship that is appropriate in the Quaker meeting – and arguably in the House of Commons too. Like a hole or a space or a lake, silence is defined by what encompasses and encloses it and by what interrupts or penetrates it. The architecture of the Meeting House, the physical orientation of those who come to worship and the oral tradition of those who rest within it bring to Quaker silence meanings that do not belong to other forms. (I borrow from biblical studies the concept of the oral tradition. It enables us to point to the stability and durability of received language.)

So liturgy is about the control of behaviour and about attaching meaning to belief and practice. But this book points particularly to Quaker liturgy and thereby to more programmed types as a level of experience. In my own tradition we have something called the liturgical silence. In the context of Quaker worship Dr Dandelion rightly prefers to talk of 'the liturgy of silence'. There are, however, significant characteristics in common. Within the Anglo-Catholic Mass the liturgical silence is kept as communicants return from the altar rail and come to rest in their pews. It is the savouring of the high point of the liturgical drama in which the faithful come closest to God and in receiving the Sacrament are made momentarily perfect. Like the silent liturgy of Quaker worship, it is a spiritual zenith.

Roger Homan
Barcombe Mills

Introduction

On Sunday morning, many young and old, rich and poor, men and women, boys and girls will go through the Church gates as the bells ring out; candles will be lit while the congregation sit to gather thoughts. Behind the scenes, priests will struggle into their chasubles, praying not to sink under the detail of the rite, a multitude of altar servers and choristers will don their clean white albs and long surplices, remembering their parts again in worried reflection readying for another performance. A gathered silence will descend, then as the organ plays and the cross is held high, all will rise as they enter public view, to represent the holy in a quire and place marked for worship. Thousands of sermons will be uttered in a variety of ecclesiastical settings, in majestic Gothic Cathedrals, suburban Victorian Churches, and in the little chapels strung out over the hills and dales of rural England. Heads will bow to pray to say 'our Father ...' Special occasions will shape rite sensibilities. Yelling babies will be hatched in holiness, couples will be matched in sacramental union and the dead will be despatched heavenwards. Receiving communion, many will return to the pew to sink and tell God that of which they cannot speak to their neighbour. In privacy in a public place, many will feel strengthened and renewed to holy purpose. At the end, all will rise for the processional hymn, and the altar party will depart, leaving those who remain to disperse. Vestments will be rehung, chalices will be put away, music re-shelved, and the lights will be put out, as the sanctuary actors depart. They leave the church with a filled emptiness and a wonder as to what passed before.

(Flanagan, 1991, pp. 1–2)

This book considers the nature of Quaker liturgy, particularly in the 'Liberal' 'unprogrammed' tradition of Quaker worship. This form of worship is very different from Flanagan's description of church rite. Worship, basically unchanged in its form since the 1650s when Quakerism began, is based in silence. Seats are arranged in a circle or square, usually in an unadorned room. Participants come into the room silently and sit where they wish. Worship usually lasts an hour. The whole time may be silent or it may be that some present share 'vocal ministry' with the rest of the group. Typically, there are three or four ministries in the hour, each lasting three or four minutes. The end of worship is signalled by the shaking of hands, initiated by one of two 'Elders', the only pre-arranged outward gesture of the whole rite. This form of Quaker worship can take place anywhere and at any time and follows no liturgical calendar, for all times and places are deemed equally sacramental. There are no pre-arranged sermons or music, no collective vocal prayer, no altar, no vestments, no celebrants or separated priesthood, nobody to lead or mediate the worship, no outward communion. Outwardly, it is bare, a minimalist service.

Flanagan lists what the sociologist observing the Catholic rite would see and comments that without an interest in what lies behind the actions and symbols, pure observation would be 'even more boring than it sounds' (1991, p. 3).

Observing this Quaker rite presents the sociologist with a different problem, that of the invisibility of the action. Participants may cough occasionally, shift in their seats, or arrive late. Those who minister stand to share their 'leadings'. If there are children associated with the 'Meeting', they may come in towards the end of worship or leave near the beginning. Otherwise, it is a fairly static liturgical form. Body language, whether eyes are open or closed, might become the desperate last attempt of a sociologist to locate meaning or difference within the group, only the words of ministry, if there is any, offering any clue to what may be happening behind this mask of silence.

Flanagan talks of liturgical silence as a potentially powerful (yet also potentially destructive) element of the Mass. For Quakers, I want to argue, elements of the Mass are subsumed into the silence. Given Rahner's definition of liturgy as the 'worship conferred to God by the church' (1975, p. 854), instead of liturgical silence, Quakers operate a silent liturgy (Baer, 1975), or a liturgy of silence:

> Liturgy belongs in the order of 'doing' (ergon), not of 'knowing' (logos). Logical thought cannot get very far with it; liturgical actions yield their intelligibility in their performance, and this performance takes place entirely at the level of sensible realities, not as exclusively material but as vehicles of overtones capable of awakening the mind and heart to acceptance of realities belonging to a different order.
>
> (Dalmais, 1987, p. 259)

Dalmais might equally have been writing about Quaker silence. Johns writes that the term 'liturgy' has its root in *leitourgia* – 'the work of the people' (1998, p. 33):

> The liturgy functions as a hermeneutic of sorts that, through its *ordo*, helps to make sense of numinous experiences. Instead of being reduced to dust by seeing the face of God, the liturgy opens the space for the worshipper to glimpse the passing shadow of the One who will be *who* he will be. Yet, the liturgy – the work of the people – also addresses those various occasions when there are no apparent traces of the One who will be *where* she will be.
>
> (Johns, 1998, p. 36)

Thus liturgy deals with both presence and perceived absence of God, the liturgy of silence finding the presence in the absence of the outward and countering the perceived absence in the depths of the silence. In this sense, silence, for the Quaker group, is not given meaning 'by virtue of it [just] being an absence' (Crumbine, 1975, 147).

Quaker silence, then, is not an easy form or a passive one. As the Quaker writer Robert Barclay wrote, 'there can be nothing more opposite to the natural will and wisdom of man than this silent waiting upon God' (2002, p. 297). Jensen claims that silence is inherently an active process, that it fulfils an activating function in the communicative process (1973, p. 255). In the silent medium of communication between God and the Meeting, Quakers claim a content that goes beyond a one-way communicative function. The silence is the very medium through which the group approaches God to seek God's will and the medium through which God's will is discerned. This emphasis on collectivity is critical to both orthodox Quaker theology and to the limitation of individualism within the worship process: '... individual experience is not sufficient, and in a meeting held under the influence of the Spirit there is a giving and receiving between its members, one helping another with or without words' (*Quaker Faith and Practice*, 1995, 2.11).

Lippard's analysis of the rhetoric of Quaker silence illuminates the orthodox perspective on the working of silent worship. She portrays a rhetorical transaction as a process of identification rather than persuasion. She argues, 'A rhetorical transaction, therefore, may be best understood at operating at some point on a continuum of conscious choice-making on the receiver's part' (1988, p. 146).

In other words, the listener has a role in the construction of the rhetorical element of the speech act. Lippard claims that in the Quaker context, a rhetorical transaction takes place within the silence. She suggests, following the Quaker view, that ministry in a 'gathered' Meeting for Worship comes from God in response to the whole Meeting:

> Not only are the 'receiver's' choices preserved in the rhetoric of the vocal ministry, they ideally determine the message. That is, the listener's attunement to a spiritual center becomes the means by which the minister is able to speak, and the guideline for forming the speech is the preservation of that common attunement. Source and receiver merge in a truly participatory rhetoric.
>
> (Lippard, 1988, p. 152)

This idealistic analysis is not matched by popular perceptions of ministry and its abuse. Lippard's view does, however, outline the logical extension of the orthodox position, one which discourages Friends from vocal contributions on the grounds that the message to be shared is universally received in an inward sense:

> In worship we have neighbours to our left and right, before and behind, yet the Eternal Presence is overall and beneath all. Worship does not consist in achieving a mental state of concentrated isolation from one's fellows. But in the depth of common worship it is as if we have found our separate lives were all one life, within whom we live and move and have our being.
>
> (*Quaker Faith and Practice*, 1995, 2.36)

Allen amplifies this notion of collectivity: 'Those who speak ... feel ... that they are not merely speaking to all present, but in a sense speaking for them' (1992, p. 5).

Thus the Quaker group finds itself in tension. Davies underlines this:

> Christianity in its reformed mode insisted that Logos, the Word, was within, not out there. It was inevitable therefore, that the extreme 17th century radicalism of the Seekers and later the Quakers should lead both to extreme positions: first, that

everyone may equally speak in worship ... and second, that nobody (at all) really
should speak because saying, speaking, is creaturely, it removes us from God.

(1988, p. 106)

The very basis of the 'free ministry' also undermines the concept. Emphasis is
placed on the silent waiting, rather than more worldly contributions: 'We highly
prize silent waiting upon the Lord in humble dependence on him. We esteem it to
be a precious part of spiritual worship, and trust that no vocal offering will ever
exclude it from its true place in our religious meetings' (*Quaker Faith and
Practice*, 1995, 2.14).

Maltz highlights this emphasis in his comparison between the role of silence in
Quaker and Pentecostal worship: 'Quakers look inward while Pentecostals look
outward. Quakers see the spirit within each individual, they contrast an inner
spiritual self with an outer actual one; they stress the silent wait for inspiration over
the inspired utterances which result' (1985, p. 134). After Shils, Quakers approach
silence as exhibiting 'charismatic' attributes (1965, p. 203). Silence is revered,
whilst the theological understanding of the role given silence militates against
speech.

This is a radical liturgy. Whilst outwardly little different from its seventeenth-
century forebear, this book looks beyond the processes of silent worship and argues
that the Quaker self-understanding of liturgical form has changed dramatically
between the seventeenth and twenty-first centuries. In particular, the book uses
'time' and 'intimacy' as two key themes that can help us get behind the silence.

This book argues that in the 1650s, early Quakers believed they were the
vanguard of an inward Second Coming of Christ, that the end of the world was
unfolding before them, and that heaven was to be created on earth as humanity
experienced the end of time and the beginning of God's realm. Outward liturgical
forms were redundant now that Pauline prophecy was being fulfilled with the
Second Coming. The 'meantime' practices of the churches, introduced to help
humanity in its relationship with God between First and Second Comings, were
anachronistic. For example, now that the Lord had come again, the injunction in 1
Corinthians to break the bread until the Lord comes again was no longer relevant.
This was a new age of the Spirit and called for new forms to mirror the new
relationship between humanity and God. Those components of the liturgy that were
still relevant were experienced inwardly, formal worship marking only an
intentionally collective expression of this permanent state.

In their intimate relationship with God, set free from sin, and living under direct
guidance from God, these first Friends claimed they were living in a potentially
permanent sacramental space. In this sense, they were living outside of time,
outside of 'the world', and outside of the material. Their lack of outward liturgy
was embedded in their sense of living as co-agents of God, in intimacy with God,
almost beyond the material. Their bodies and lives were merely sites and channels
to communicate the word of God, the living Christ, to others. Their intimate

liturgical form was expressed physically through presence (individually) and absence (of liturgical props) but pointed to a particular and intimate relationship with the transcendent located in a particular moment of endtime chronology. These understandings are explored in Chapters 1 and 2. Chapter 3 considers how this intimacy with God gave Friends an alternate sense of being as well as time. It goes on to chart the theological shifts in Quakerism in the eighteenth and nineteenth centuries, beginning with the publication of Robert Barclay's influential *Apology* in the 1670s. Thus, the term 'early' or 'first' Friends is used to refer to those writing in the 1650s and 1660s.

What Barclay did was modify early Quaker understandings of where they saw themselves within a biblical understanding of time whilst retaining an intellectually coherent argument for unprogrammed worship and a lack of outward meantime liturgical practices. Using the same scriptural verses as the early Quakers, Barclay maintained a theological understanding of intimacy with God, albeit a different one from the first Friends. This relationship of intimacy played itself out in a more cautious and anxious way within an apostate world these 'Quietist' Friends were now wary of. The lack of outward meantime liturgical practices to help Friends remain faithful was compensated by a whole range of 'peculiarities' such as endogamy, plain dress and plain speech.

The nineteenth century saw further change. This is explored in Chapter 4. The influential theologian of this period was Joseph John Gurney, more Evangelical in his thinking than Barclay, but still wedded to the unprogrammed form. Indeed, many of his arguments about the right holding of worship, baptism and the Lord's Supper, were close to those used by Barclay. He too talked of the Quaker intimacy with God in terms of the First Coming rather than the Second, but he also placed Scripture as having at least equal authority to revelation, his major departure from Barclay. Whilst this didn't bring about liturgical change in Britain, it accommodated Revival influence on Evangelical Friends in the US. There, some Friends moved increasingly away from the formalism of Quietistic silent worship to more expressive responses to a relationship of intimacy they still held as central. In time, in response to the needs of huge numbers of converts, these Friends adopted a pastoral system that was to lead to programming. These pastoral Friends were of two sorts, revivalist and modernist. Some of the former found themselves isolated in their bid to obtain the toleration of water baptism. The latter were to wage a campaign to retain a distinctive Quakerism but one that was more open to the world. This was successful in creating a particular form of Quaker Evangelicalism in the United States and a Liberal Quakerism on both sides of the Atlantic.

This Liberal Quakerism gave experience greater authority than Scripture, emphasised the idea that Quakerism should be of its age and always open to new ideas, and instituted a system of progressive revelation whereby new revelation had a greater authority than old. This combination of characteristics did not entail a necessary theology and the assumed Christianity of its founders was to be replaced in time by diverse interpretations of the experience that was now central. Liturgical reform did not follow but the basis of it is very different from the unprogrammed Quakerism of before.

Twenty-first-century Liberal Quakers do not talk about the Second Coming. Many are not Christian and few claim the kind of life-changing experiences their seventeenth-century forebears expressed through their journals, tracts and preaching. However, this tradition of Quakerism has consistently decided to maintain a liturgical form based on the experience and theology of the Second Coming while, from as early as the 1670s, no longer claiming the experience itself. Chapter 5 looks at present-day practice across different traditions. Chapters 6 and 7 explore the way in which the unprogrammed liturgy is managed and understood today by Liberal Friends.

It is argued that the understanding of liturgy mirrors in part the change in understanding of God. As God has become humanised and internalised in the twentieth century, so this 'liturgy of silence' is seen to be an individual event pointing not to an intimate transcendence but to an intimate immanence, or even, in some cases, self-divinity. Quakers in this framework have also moved 'out of time', though not because of the imminent end of historical time, but because only the present is real or can be trusted. The future is no longer colliding with the present (Dandelion et al., 1998, p. 252), rather it has ceased to exist.

This book ultimately argues that while the first Friends derived a radical liturgy of intimacy with God from within a radical understanding of time, intimacy for Liberal Friends has become the dominant organising principle and has become de-coupled from its original source. Rather, this radical sense of time has been lost, intimacy instead self-evident and self-validating. For Programmed Friends, the same abstraction of worship is not there. For them, the liturgy is grounded in a particular understanding of intimate Christianity, a basis foreign to unprogrammed Liberal Friends.

Little has been written on the sociology of liturgy, other than Kieran Flanagan's important and influential book (1991) and Martin Stringer's (1999) and Elizabeth Collinge-Hill's (2001) interesting work on the ethnography of worship; very little has been written on Quaker liturgy. Richard Bauman's and Douglas Gwyn's work is however seminal. I am also indebted to Michele Tarter, Timothy Peat and Peter Collins, on whose work I have been able to build, as well as Richard Fenn's insights into time, which first led me to think about Quaker theology in terms of its relationship to time. The friendship and support of these scholars has also been invaluable.

This book was completed in Oregon and I owe a debt of gratitude to Reedwood Friends Church for giving me the space and time to do this work. I am also indebted to the participants on a course I ran at Woodbrooke, the Quaker Study Centre in Birmingham, and to members of the 2003 Quaker Studies Research Summer School, who gave me a chance to air some of the propositions of this book and who reflected them back to me in a clarified form. Amongst that number, I need to particularly thank Jennie Barnsley, Gill Grimshaw, Betty Haglund, Edwina

Newman and Susan Robson. I also thank all those Friends who have kept asking me how it was going and who phoned and e-mailed me during my sojourn in the US. Deborah Shaw was particularly kind in helping me collect data, and Paul Anderson increased my understanding manyfold over one memorable breakfast.

I have been continually grateful over the last 18 years for the mentorship of Roger Homan, and I am privileged that he has agreed to contribute the Foreword.

In the last years, working and joking alongside Doug Gwyn has fuelled much of my academic work and this book is dedicated to him.

CHAPTER 1

The End of Time and the Beginning of Quakerism

'hours, days, months, which are the rags of time'
('The Sun-Rising', John Donne, cited in Cope, 2001, p. 36)

John Binns has written of Orthodox liturgy that 'it is the meeting of God and humanity and at it the nature of the Church is most clearly seen and experienced' (2002, p. 40). In a sense, this is true of Quakerism too except that the early Quaker senses of time and intimacy placed their liturgical form on a continuum with the everyday, that is, the liturgical form collectivised the individual experience. Whereas Binns can write that the Eucharist made the Church 'complete and whole' (2002, p. 41), Quaker worship reflected the nature of the Church as realised inwardly in the everyday life. This chapter explores these particular understandings of time and intimacy as frameworks for approaching liturgy in a Quaker context.

Time

Richard Fenn has been key in helping sociologists of religion think more about the nature of time as a critical factor in religious discourse. In particular, his books, *The Persistence of Purgatory* (1995), *The End of Time* (1997), and *Time Exposure* (2001) use the organisation and commodification of time by secular and religious society as theoretical frameworks within which to explore the changing relationship between humanity and their sense of their ability to shape their religious life and destiny.

In his 1995 work, Fenn argues that western culture has become inordinately interested in time. Not only has time become constructed and ordered in new ways in the last centuries but it has become more important. Time today is something many feel the lack of, but it is also a significant aspect of consumer culture. For those who have 'disposable time', those who feel its lack may be victims of their own inability to discriminate between opportunities: not having enough time can be a crisis of freedom. We can buy time by paying others to do jobs for us, organise our time by diary or computer, use time more 'effectively', for example, by multi-tasking or through mobile devices which allow us to extend workspace into public arenas, such as trains or airports. Time for work is less segregated than it used to be. The use of time itself has become extended, with a concomitant rise in expectations about output. Ownership of our time is an emblem of freedom and therefore of success and happiness. Time has been centralised and rationalised, ordered around fixed systems (for example, Greenwich Mean Time).

We 'make up for lost time', 'run out of time' and 'do time' if we transgress. Waiting, not 'using' time, becomes the punishment for actions judged as wrong by secular society. At the same time, Fenn argues, the invention of purgatory in the thirteenth century and since plays into our fears about running out of time by offering us the possibility or even probability of extra time in order to make the final and necessary adjustments to our spiritual balance sheet (1995). Thus time becomes the means, in this case extra time as the gift of the Church, but also part of the calculations for individual salvation. Fenn argues that it is this very proximity of individual to eternal life that makes time so serious. The fact that purgatory runs on the same system of time as on earth gives it an added realism, and terror:

> ... Biblical religion has long made time a proving ground of the spirit and of divine intentions. The end-time was often, if not always, approaching, and occasionally the end was even at hand. It was with the doctrine of purgatory, however, that time took on an added seriousness far beyond that of the apocalyptic. Time in this world became continuous with the after-life, since, in purgatory, clocks tick and the hours and days pass on exactly the same schedule as on earth. When this life is subsumed within heaven, of course, time stands still. It is when the grace of heaven is near at hand, even while the hours and days pass with apparent indifference, that time becomes serious.
> (Fenn, 1995, p. 16)

Schweitzer claimed that the history of Christianity was about the delay of the parousia, the Second Coming (1968, p. 360). Johns notes in this regard:

> Unlike the notion of cyclical time, evident in some traditions, the Christian conception of sacred time follows a spiral pattern; Christian sacred time does not require the performance of the rite for the actual event to occur or for the *illud tempus* (time of origin) to be reactualized. Rather, the spiral progresses along a linear path moving ever closer toward the *telos* of the community's eschatological hope.
> (1998, p. 35)

As Revelation 10:6 suggests of the endtime, 'there should be time no longer.'

As the history of the life of a Christian is about gaining the eternal life Fenn talks of, so Christianity has had to calculate and recalculate the time when time would end for everyone. While nurturing the individual Christian's life, the Church has also needed to be ready for the endtime, the coming of the Kingdom, the end of human time. Thus it has been caught in a complex of schedules, of remembrance of time not to be forgotten, of the present-day life of the Church members and their path to salvation, and the future time when heaven will be realised on earth and humanity will be in a final post-lapsarian state, a true intimacy with the atemporal God, prefigured in the Gospel of Matthew, the letters of Paul, and the book of Revelation amongst other scriptural texts.

As the timing of the Second Coming became less clear and obviously still a *future-* event, the Church needed to develop a theology of the interim, a theology of the 'meantime'. Paul's letters offer a changing view of the timing of the moment when the earnest will be realised in full, when the experience of the risen Christ that Paul has been given will be available to all. The development of a meantime theology therefore needed to look backward to the intersection of heaven and earth, realised through the life, death and resurrection of Christ, and forward to the final intersection. It also needed to help humanity remain faithful and remain expectant. The history of Christianity has been about the meantime within this biblical framework of time.

Figure 1.1 is based on Timothy Peat's scholarship on Paul and offers an understanding of the Biblical understanding of time, particularly a Pauline one (Dandelion et al., 1998, p. 157). On the left-hand side of the diagram, we see that the Fall initiates a separation between God and humanity, between heaven and earth, the mythic and the mundane, God's time and human time. Humanity lives separated from God, living by the law that mediates God's guidance, living as 'children' in a continual struggle with sin and shortcoming.

The life, death and resurrection of Christ is an intersection of these two realms, of heaven and earth, and through this, Paul, the last to see the risen Christ and 'born out of due time' (1 Cor. 15:8), is given the clear sense of what has been promised to the whole of humanity. The encounter with the risen Christ gives Paul a foretaste of the global transformation that will come for everyone, the inheritance of the people

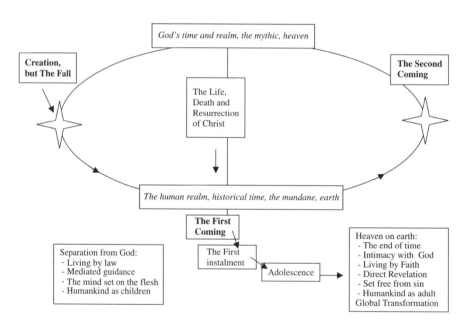

Figure 1.1 A biblical understanding of time

of God. Paul looks to a place when heaven and earth will again be as one, when humanity will be in intimacy with God, living with the same transparency to God as Jesus did, living by faith not by the law, set free from sin. It will be the end of time, the beginning of the kingdom of God realised on earth. It will be the culmination of God's plan for humanity, the realisation of global 'adulthood', an Eden without the possibility of Fall.

This idea of awaiting an endtime is what required strategies for the meantime, humanity in adolescence (Dandelion et al., 1998, p. 84), able to see what adulthood may look like and having glimpses of the experience from time to time, but still needing guidance and help. The Church itself is clear on this. The Vatican II papers state, ' . . . the pilgrim church, in its sacraments and institutions, which belong to this present age, carries the mark of this world which will pass, and she herself takes her place among the creatures which groan and travail yet and await the revelation of the sons of God [cf. Rom. 8:19–22]' (Flannery, 1975, p. 408).

Sacraments, along with other aspects of church life, such as set-apart buildings, a separated priesthood, special times and seasons (a Christian calendar), are temporary:

> The Christian Eucharist remains the contrary of modern time, as the site where time continues to arrive from eternity. Christ's eucharistic presence arrives from past and future, constituting the present moment through the church's recollection and anticipation of what is promised: the ever-renewed arrival of God's eternity in Christ. The Eucharist eternalizes time, as to that which arrives and passes away in order to return again, bearing eternal life with it. The eucharistic celebration teaches the church how to wait upon the arrival of God's gift of time.
>
> (Loughlin, 2000, p. 709)

The eucharist is part of an interim theology, an instruction on how to wait, on how the Church is to 'do time'. As Dix states, 'there is no more effective way of keeping the plain Christian man and woman in mind of the elementary facts of Christian doctrine than the perpetual round of the Hours of the Passion set in the ordered sequence of the liturgical seasons' (1946, p. 333).

For the first Quakers, a new state had come:

> Behold, the days come saith the Lord, that I will make a new covenant with the house of Israel, and with the house of Judah: Not according to the covenant that I made with their fathers in the day that I took them by the hand to bring them out of the land of Egypt; which my covenant they broke, although I was an husband unto them, saith the Lord: But this shall be the covenant that I will make with the house of Israel; After those days, saith the Lord, I will put my law in their inward parts, and write in their hearts; and will be their God, and they shall be my people. And they shall teach no more every man his neighbour, and every man his brother, saying Know the lord: for they shall all know me, from the least of them unto the greatest of them, saith the Lord: for I will forgive their iniquity, and I will remember their sin no more.
>
> (Jeremiah 31:31–4)

Powerful personal and intimate religious experience convinced them of a direct connection with God, an inward experience of the Second Coming of Christ, and the beginning of the end of the world. In this sense, early Friends can be placed at the end of time in Figure 1.2.

> I was moved to open my mouth and lift up my voice aloud in the mighty power of the Lord, and to tell them the mighty Day of the Lord was coming upon all deceitful merchandise and ways, and to call them all to repentance and a turning to the Lord God, and his Spirit within them, for it to teach them and lead them, and tremble before the mighty God of heaven and earth, for his mighty Day was coming.
>
> (Fox, 1952, p. 121)

The Second Coming, the end of time, was unfolding, a realising eschatology, and this group symbolised and experienced the potential for global transformation. As Gwyn states, 'The inward experience of the risen Christ is an advance view of the consummation of the outward in history' (1986, p. 116). Time comes to be seen from a different perspective:

> Fox describes the life of faith – *out* of time (or history) as a primary reference, yet still *in* time and *through* time … this interface between time (the old, present age) and the everlasting (the new, coming age) is the place of the cross. Fox's description of this entry into the new age, even while one is still engaged with the old age, suggests a

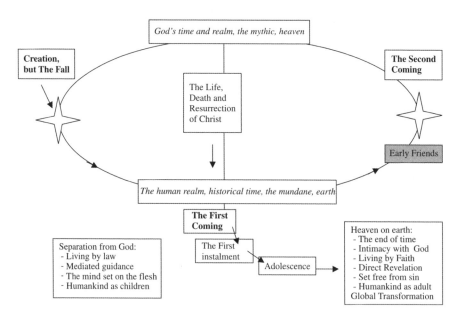

Figure 1.2 A biblical understanding of time and early Friends

relationship between the two in which they do not simply join end to end (as one year succeeds another) but in which the new age diverges from the old into a new dimension of experience.

(Gwyn, 1986, p. 117)

The world was captive and time symbolises and represents this captivity. The worldly was begun in time and will end in time, but Fox claims to work from a sense of truth outside of time or from before time (prelapsarian) for the coming of the Kingdom which will be everlasting, that is, without end or outside of the constraints of time (ibid.):

> All Friends everywhere, meet together, and in the measure of God's spirit wait, that with it all your minds may be guided up to God, that ye may all come to know how ye may walk with him in his wisdom, that it may be justified of you, and ye in it be preserved up to God, and be glorified. And Friends, meet together, and know one another in that which is eternal, which was before the world was. For knowing one another only in the letter and the flesh differs you little from the beasts of the field for what they know, they know naturally. But all knowing one another in the light which was before the world was, this differs you from the beasts of the field, and from the world's knowledge and brings you to know one another in the elect seed which was before the world was.
>
> (Fox, 1990, vol. 7, p. 141)

Fenn points out that 'doing time' or waiting may not be just a consequence of social power, for example, within a prison system, it may also reflect a lack of synchronisation between societal life, or indeed the delay from infancy to adulthood (1995, p. 2). All three possibilities are relevant here. Early Quakers experienced time in all three ways: as prisoners, persecuted under the Blasphemy Act of 1650, or the Quaker Act 1662, or subsequent Conventicle Acts; as those awaiting all parts of society to accept God's invitation to a new covenant, and, within Pauline prophecy, for humanity to move through its adolescence to the mature intimacy with God now available (Dandelion et al., 1998, pp. 82–3). There is also the imprisonment of the seed within: 'So the ministers of the Spirit must minister to the Spirit that is transgressed and in prison, which hath been in captivity in everyone; whereby with the same Spirit people must be led out of captivity up to God ...' (Fox, 1952, p. 263).

Gwyn's study of Fox shows how he always tried to encourage his followers to feel themselves not only incarnating Christ but also to sense the move away from calendrical time that accompanied such an experience (1981, pp. 91–2; 1986, pp. 116–18): 'And ye who are the Lord's, are not your own; but they who are in their own time, see not the time which is in the Father's hand; their time is always, and they do their own works, and not the works of God, which the son of God did' (Fox, 1990, vol. 7, p. 133).

Fox offered a warning to the bellringers who, as such, acted as timekeepers: ' ... prize your time now while you have it ... The time will come when you will say you had time, when it is past. Oh, look at the love of God now while you have time ... Oh, consider, time is precious' (Nickalls, 1952, p. 55). The Day of the Lord was unfolding for all. All would be judged. Fox offers a final warning to those still captive and caught up in ways which might hinder the potential already realised by the Quakers.

Davies talks of the ritual generation of time:

> Christian churches have been responsible for giving the passing days, weeks, and years distinctive significance, and through their ritual events has emerged a keen sense of time, especially of '*kairos*-time', periods of divine significance for humanity. Ritual actually generates and maintains these perspectives ...
>
> (2002, p. 188)

Davies points out that the Church of England's *Common Worship* includes the concept of 'ordinary time', time without 'seasonal emphasis' (*Common Worship*, 2002, p. 532). For early Quakers, there was neither seasonal emphasis nor ordinary time. In 1680, Fox commented on special set apart times and seasons. Vital 'till he come' (1 Cor. 11:26), the only day to observe now was 'The Everlasting Day, the Day of Christ Jesus' (Gwyn, 1981, p. 80). All life was now potentially 'out of time', and soon all time would end. Time had ended and was ending. The lack of ritual events, for them, marked this particular and final kairos moment:

> The vital and triumphant message of Quakerism is that *the work has already begun*. Fox expresses this repeatedly in his proclamations that Christ 'is come and coming to reign', 'the church in her glory is appeared and appearing', 'the mighty day of the Lord is come, and coming to all the world, and his salvation shall be known to all the ends of the earth', 'now is Babylon confounded and confounding.' With this figure of speech, he grounds ultimate future in unfolding present.
>
> (Gwyn, 1986, p. 206)

Intimacy

According to Somerville, access to God may give an individual 'feelings of remoteness, "otherness" and dependence' before such power (Somerville, 1992, p. 7). As Fenn suggests, 'there is in religion, then, a peculiar combination of experiences; what is beyond, distant, absent is felt as present; what is clearly present is experienced in terms of its absence or transcendence' (Fenn, 1995, p. 34).

For the early Friends, this dualism was clear. What is interesting is that they did not feel bound by their outward mortality. They simply became part of 'somewhere else', a distinct space (a phenomenon returned to in Chapter 3). Access to God, through Christ the Word, resulted in an intimacy from which they looked back on where they had been before and on the souls who they hoped would follow in their experience.

In 1647, George Fox first realised the possibility of direct access:

> When all my hopes in them [dissenters] and in all men were gone, so that I had
> nothing outwardly to help me, nor could tell what to do, then, Oh then, I heard a voice
> which said, 'There is one, even Christ Jesus, that can speak to thy condition,' and
> when I heard it my heart did leap for joy.
>
> (Fox, 1952, p. 11)

In 1648, this was followed up by the next stage of his 'convincement' experience, a regenerative and perfecting experience following the illumination of, and repentance for, former sins. Convincement meant literally conviction (Pickvance, 1989, p. 63). Friends were convicted of their fallen state but equally given the power to move on to a new life in which sin could be resisted:

> Now I was come up in spirit through the flaming sword into the paradise of God. All
> things were new, and all creation gave another smell unto me than before, beyond
> what words can utter. I knew nothing but pureness, and innocency, and righteousness,
> being renewed up into the image of God by Christ Jesus, so that I say I was come up to
> the state of Adam which he was in before he fell ... But I was immediately taken up
> in spirit to see into another or more steadfast state than Adam's in innocency, even
> into a state in Christ Jesus that should never fall.
>
> (Fox, 1952, p. 27)

Here, we have the return to Eden through the flaming sword of Genesis 3, into a state of all things being new (Rev. 21:1), but also the passage to a higher state, the sinlessness prophesied by Paul (Dandelion et al., 1998, p. 83).

Ultimately, this experience would lead the convinced to gather together, and in the years which followed, to call 'the world' towards a new mode of religious experience. Fox was critical of those who looked to outward means to the Kingdom, such as the Fifth Monarchists (Gwyn, 1981, p. 86). The new covenant was not to be found outwardly, neither did it require any intermediary. Additionally, it was open to everyone, men and women and children. By 1660, there were perhaps 60,000 Quakers in Britain (Braithwaite, 1912, p. 512).

It is not clear how many of these converts had the same vivid and full experience of Fox but many of the other early leaders of the movement have left accounts of their convincement narratives.

For Penington, the initial experience of intimacy was too great:

> And indeed at last (when my nature was almost spent, and the pit of despair was even
> closing its mouth upon me) mercy sprang, and deliverance came, and the Lord my
> God owned me, and sealed his love unto me, and light sprang within me, which made
> not only the Scriptures, but the very outward creatures glorious in my eye, so that
> every thing was sweet and pleasant and light-some round about me. But soon I felt,
> that this estate was too high and glorious for me, and was not able to abide in it, it so
> overcame my natural spirits; wherefore, blessing the name of the Lord for his great
> goodness to me, I prayed unto him to take that from me which I was not able to bear,

and to give me such a proportion of his light and presence, as was suitable to my present state, and might fit me for his service. Whereupon this was presently removed from me ...

(Penington, 1996, p. 101)

Later, his full convincement was equally distressing:

... I was smitten, broken, and distressed by the Lord, confounded in my worship, confounded in my knowledge, stripped of all in one day ... and was matter of amazement to all that beheld me. I lay open and naked to all that would inquire of me, and strive to search out what might be the cause the Lord should deal so with me ... My soul remembereth the wormwood and gall, the exceeding bitterness of that state, and is still humbled in me the remembrance of it before the Lord. Oh how I did wish with Job, that I might come before him, and bowingly plead with him; for indeed I had no sense of any guilt upon me, but was sick of love towards him, and as one violently rent from the bosom of his beloved! Oh, how gladly would I have met with death! For I was weary all the day long, and afraid of the night, and weary also of the night-season, and afraid of the ensuing day. I remember my grievous and bitter mournings to the Lord; how often did I say, O Lord, why hast thou forsaken me? Why hast thou broken me to pieces? I had no delight but thee, no desire after any but thee. My heart was bent wholly to serve thee and thou hast even fitted me (as appeared to my sense) by many deep exercises and experiences for thy service; why dost thou make me thus miserable? ... In this condition I wandered up and down from mountain to hill, from one sort to another, with a cry in my spirit, Can ye tell news of my beloved? Where doth he dwell? Where doth he appear?

(Penington, 1996, p. 102)

Penington was later still led out of this state by an inward sense of the holy power of the Lord falling upon him (ibid.). In both instances of Penington's experience, and with Fox too, regeneration comes after a period of deep despair. Crisp's experience is similar:

A swift sword was drawn against that wisdom and comprehending mind, and a strong hand gave the stroke, and I was hewn down like a tall cedar, that at once comes down to the ground. But then, oh the woe, misery and calamity that opened upon me! Yea, even the gates of hell and destruction stood open, and I saw myself nigh falling thereinto, my hope and faith, and all fled from me. I had no prop left me to rest on. The tongue that was as a river, was now like a dry desert; the eye that would, or at least desired to see everything, was now so blind, that I could see nothing certainly, but my present undone and miserable state ... oh how doleful was my nights, and sorrowful was my days! My delighte withered even in wife and children, and in all things; and the glory of the whole world pased away like a scroll that s burnt with fire; and I saw nothing left in the world to give me any comfort. My sun lost her light, and my moon was darkened, and the stars of my course were fallen, that I knew no more how to direct my way, but was as one forsaken in a howling desert in the darkest night.

(Barbour and Roberts, 1973 [1694], pp. 203–04)

Also typical of convincement narratives is the long period of searching these early Quaker converts experienced. Fox talks of meeting with different groups and

Howgill's account (Barbour and Roberts, 1973, pp. 167–79) charts his shifting allegiances until the point he met George Fox:

> And immediately, as soon as I heard one declare, (one whose name is not known to the world, but written in the Lamb's book of life forever, in eternal record forever) as soon as I heard him declare that the Light of Christ in man was the way to Christ, I believed the eternal word of truth, and that of God in my conscience sealed to it. And so, not only I, but many hundred more, who thirsted after the Lord, but were betrayed by the wisdom of the serpent; we were all seen to be off the foundation, and all mouths were stopped in the dust. We all stood as condemned in our selves and all saw our nakedness, and were all ashamed, though our glory was great in the world's eye, but all was vanity.
>
> (Barbour and Roberts, 1973 [1655], p. 173)

Howgill's convincement followed soon after:

> My eyes were opened, and all the things that I had ever done were brought to remembrance and the ark of the testament was opened, and there was thunder and lightning and great hail. And then the trumpet of the Lord was sounded, and then nothing but war and rumor of war, and the dreadful power of the Lord fell on me: plague, and pestilence, and famine, and earthquake, and fear and terror, for the sights I saw with my eyes: and that which I heard with my ears, sorrow and pain. And in the morning I wished it had been evening, and in the evening I wished it had been morning and I had no rest, but trouble on every side. And all that ever I had done was judged and condemned, all things were accursed; whether I did eat, or drink, or restrain, I was accursed. Then the lions suffered hunger, and the seals were opened, and seven thunders uttered their voices ... I became a perfect fool, and knew nothing, as a man distracted; all was overturned, and I suffered loss of all. In all that I ever did, I saw it was in the accursed nature. And then something in me cried: 'Just and true is his judgement!' My mouth was stopped, I dared not make mention of his name, I knew not God. And as I bore the indignation of the Lord, something rejoiced, the serpent's head began to be bruised, and the witnesses which were slain were raised ... And as I did give up all to judgement, the captive came forth out of prison and rejoiced, and my heart was filled with joy. I came to see him whom I had pierced, and my heart as broken, and the blood of the prophets I saw slain, and a great lamentation. Then I saw the cross of Christ, and stood in it, and the enmity slain on it. And the new man was made ... the holy law of God was revealed unto me and written on my heart.
> (Ibid.)

Penington and Crisp and Howgill all struggle with time, wishing morning was evening and evening was morning. Time drags in the early stages of the convincement experience, but culminates in a sense of eternal life. Howgill comes to see how all he has done previously has been part of the ongoing crucifixion of Christ but that now he can stand in the place of the cross, the seals opened, after Revelation, the Serpent's head bruised (after Gen. 3:15, Rom. 16:20), the place of the inward Second Coming (after Jer. 31:31–4), a new man: 'Self must be denied, and that you must deny if you receive of him, that he may be all, and you nothing' (Barbour and Roberts, 1973 [1655], p. 175).

It was the end of waiting, the end of separated times for the Church and for the rest of life. It was heaven realised on earth, a continual intimacy of love and obedience. As Burrough stated:

> The worship of God in itself is this. It is a walking with God, and a living with him in converse and fellowship therein, and to do the truth, and speak the truth: this is the true worship of God, where the mind is girded with the spirit of truth, and the presence of the Lord felt at all time, and his fear in the heart of people and his counsel stood in, and his covenant felt, which unites to the Lord in spirit, this is the true worship of God; and it is without respect of time or things.
>
> (Burrough, 1672, p. 474)

Setting a worship time was only the formalisation of the experience of the means to salvation, or of salvation's expression: a collective response to God's power breaking in through the inward silence of daily life (Bauman, 1983, p. 127). Friends met on first day (Sunday) out of convenience, but also often mid-week too (Woods, 2002, Chapter 3). Equally, place became an expanded concept. Friends met in streets or fields, on hilltops, able to worship anywhere (Woods, 2002, Chapter 2).

Doug Gwyn explains how early Friends felt themselves united within a new covenantal reality, a participational 'covenant of Light' as opposed to the propositional Puritan covenant of Grace. The covenant of Grace located God's law as both written on the heart of the elect and stated in Scripture (Gwyn, 1995, p. 73). The covenant of Light was a covenant of a life with God, outside of credal formulation, following Jeremiah 31:31–4 (Gwyn, 1995, p. 108). Scripture confirmed the inward intimacy and revelation through the inward Christ but was not the Word of God, for Christ was the living Word (Bauman, 1983, p. 26). Gwyn quotes Howgill: 'We were knit together not by any external covenant or form, but by the covenant of life with God, a strong obligation, or bond upon all our spirits, unites as one to another ... in the unity of the Spirit and the bond of peace' (Gwyn, 1995, p. 108).

Burrough also emphasises the collective aspect to this new experience: 'The Covenant of God is Unity betwixt God and man, and a binding each to the other, to serve each other, the one bound to obey, submit, and worship; the other to blesse, and keep, and lead, and preserve' (Burrough, 1657, in Gwyn, 1995, p. 108). As Gwyn states:

> Provisions of this covenant include; no teacher but God, who teaches *all*; a just law within to condemn transgression; a pure spirit within to rule and guide in all things; no priest but Jesus Christ; no light but the light of the lamb; no knowledge of God but by the revelation of Jesus Christ; no traditions and observances (established church forms).
>
> (Gwyn, 1995, p. 109)

Creasey highlights the use of spatial terms in early Quaker writing, in particular, distinctions between 'inward' and 'outward' (1962). Creasey claims that Fox used the term 'outward' to refer to formal and conventional Christianity and 'inward' to refer to 'a transforming and creative personal acquaintance with and relation to Christ in the Spirit' (1962, p. 3). Graves find this pattern in early Quaker sermons as well (1972, p. 253). The inward does not eliminate the need for the outward but is a necessary and vital part of the new covenant: 'Let us not be Outward but also inward Christians' (*Harmony of Divine and Heavenly Doctrines*, 1723, p. 197).

Only later, in more apologetic writing do Penn and Barclay appear to create a hierarchy of modes of revelation between inward and outward (Graves, 1972, p. 253). Graves suggests that in this way, both historical and spiritual Christianity are emphasised. These Quakers are thus still 'in' time and yet 'out' of it.

I want to draw out this contrast between outward and inward into a contrast between the captivity of outward religion and the intimacy of the inward, between the captivity of the meantime, of 'doing time', and the intimacy of the inward experience. I want to thus also suggest that we can use intimacy to denote an atemporal state, a state out of time, in the way that lovers might 'lose track of time' or find their experience transcends the mundane including schedule. Intimacy here becomes meta-temporal. The Quaker experience is thus temporal, in that they engage with the world, and meta-temporal in their relationship with Christ the Word. All is headed towards a global meta-temporality where heaven is realised on earth and time and history, and the Church as it has been known, ends.

This contrasts, as we shall see in the next chapter, with the more outward liturgical focus of other parts of Christianity. There, the liturgy points towards this intimacy, the coming of heaven on earth, or even offers a temporary installation of this state (Binns, 2002, p. 43), creating an outward expression of the presence of Christ in the midst of the worshipping group. Quakers began from a different understanding of the realisation of heaven on earth, that is, that it is present and ongoing, not temporary or a future prospect; they experienced and expressed this realisation inwardly rather than outwardly, resulting in a minimalist external liturgical form.

The seventeenth-century Quaker sermons and writings continually allude to this outward/inward, captivity/intimacy dichotomy. The attitude to the naming of days and months symbolises this stance of being 'in time but not of it': early Quakers called days and months by number so as not to use pagan and Roman nomenclature. Thus, Sunday was first day, Monday second, etc. This testimony is still evident in parts of Quakerism today ('First Day school' is still common) but has generally fallen away in the last century. When the British calendrical system was revised in 1752, the reordering of the months so that 'the year' began in January rather than March gave rise to even more criticism of the worldly system now that, for example, the new ninth month was called September, that is, the seventh. Not only was it pagan, it wasn't even accurate. Still, using numbers for months might have led to much confusion amongst Friends, hence a lengthy minute on the matter (*Book of Extracts*, 1783, pp. 45–54).

Separated and human time was finished with, separated space an anachronism, ideas of alienation from God inappropriate. Ultimately, it was the end of humanity as a group separated from God. All would be ordained to act as the royal priesthood for God's loving purposes. As Howgill wrote:

> The Lord of heaven and earth we found to be near at hand, and, as we waited upon him in pre silence, our mind out of all things, His heavenly presence appeared in our assemblies, when there was no language, tongue nor speech from any creature. The kingdom of heaven did gather us and catch us all, as in a net, and His heavenly power at one time drew many hundreds to land. We came to know a place to stand in and what to wait in; and the Lord appeared daily to us, to our astonishment, amazement, and great admiration, insomuch that we often said one unto another, with great joy of heart: 'What, is the kingdom of God come to be with men? And will he take up His tabernacle among the sons of men, as He did of old? And what? Shall we, that were reckoned as the outcasts of Israel, have this honour of glory communicated amongst others, as amongst men?' And from that day forward, our hearts were knit unto the Lord and one another in true and fervent love, in the covenant of Life with god; and that was a strong bond upon our spirits, which united us one to another. (Burrough, 1672, prelim leaf e 3, as abridged in *Quaker Faith and Practice*, 1995, 19.08)

The early Quaker understanding of time, that is, the end of time, carried with it an implicit and realised intimacy with God. The two were intertwined. The new state of collective intimacy convinced Friends of their place in the biblical understanding of time, and their sense of time explained and legitimated their sense of intimacy. An inward understanding of prophecy and an inward experience of the signs of prophecy was central to early Quakerism. This radical reading of the time(s) underpinned the Quaker approach to liturgical form and set it apart from the rest of Christianity. We look at the Quaker approach to baptism, eucharist, and the ministry in the next chapter.

CHAPTER 2

The Liturgy of Silence

Timothy Peat has characterised this early Quaker combination of experiential and theological certainties as the fulfilment of Paul's prophecy (Dandelion et al., 1998, pp. 107–15). Paul points to a time of global transformation accompanying the Second Coming of Christ, in which humankind is guided directly by God gathered into community (1 Cor. 12:12) and set free from sin. This was exactly the experience of early Friends and was the framework for the diagrams used in the preceding chapter.

Alternatively, Douglas Gwyn sees Fox's teaching as particularly connected to an interpretation of the book of Revelation. Gwyn argues that Revelation was 'the only book of the Bible to receive an extended, point-by-point interpretation in his writings' (Gwyn, 1986, p. 186). Moreover, the language of Revelation infuses all of Fox's writings. There is an urgency to Fox's prophecy based on his reading of his times within the frame of Revelation.

'The great people to be gathered in white raiment' (Fox, 1952, p. 104), which Fox sees in his vision on the evening after he climbed Pendle Hill in 1652, mirrors those elders around the throne in white raiment in Revelation 4, and more generally the faithful who shall be clothed in white raiment (Rev. 3:5, 18; 10:8, 14) and those who had 'washed their robes and made them white in the blood of the lamb' (Rev. 7:14).

Fox understands the Apocalypse of John experientially and empathically, as if they share the same vantage point over the coming endtimes: 'The judgement upon the earth that are described by John with the breaking of the seven seals are known in the practice of waiting upon the Lord. Here the birth according to the flesh is silenced and judged, so that the birth according to the Spirit may be raised up' (Gwyn, 1986, p. 186).

Quaking in worship was the quaking of the earth in people's hearts so that the seed could be loosed from captivity and raised up, after Revelation 6:12–14 and the breaking of the sixth seal (Gwyn, 1986, p. 187). This is not a new experience but one experienced before by the prophets and apostles (Joel 2:2, 10, Isa. 66:2, Heb. 12:21, 26, 27). The revelation of Christ comes after the breaking of the seventh seal that is followed by half an hour of silence in heaven. In the silence, the old world passes away and the new is born. Those living in this encounter with Christ experience this transition out of time into the kingdom (Gwyn, 1986, p. 187). This is not a private experience however, the personal encounter suggesting and anticipating the formation of a holy nation (1 Pet. 2:9), the true church (Gwyn, 1986, p. 189), and its battle alongside God for global transformation. People would need to choose which side they were on (Gwyn, 1981, p. 62).

Fox is clear of the apostasy of the Church he has grown up with. The paid clergy, the preaching of sin, the false teaching he hears are all signs of a Church of false prophets (Matt. 7:15, 24:11, 24) and the old covenant (Gal. 5:1–6, Heb. 9:10–15) that has chased the true church into the wilderness (Rev. 12:6) (Gwyn, 1986, p. 190). Fox and other early Friends liken the relationship of State and Church as similar to Babylon riding on the Beast, referred to by John (Rev. 17:3). It may have an outward splendour but it lacks the realised power of God which will help the true Church come forth (Gwyn, 1986, p. 192). His criticism was not confined to only certain groups: Howgill was to write of the Separatists that they had not fully escaped Babylon but were still in its suburbs (Gwyn, 1986, p. 193).

The Quakers saw themselves as the true (faithful) Church, the holy nation, gathering as in Revelation 14:4, 5 to follow the Lamb and wage and win the Lamb's War, a spiritual war (2 Cor. 10:3, Eph. 6:10–17) waged by preaching the true ways which will bring the world's people away from apostasy and false prophets (Rev. 18:4, 11). Fox claimed:

> ... and now the gospel of God is known, the power of God, and now is the mystery of the fellowship [Eph. 3:9] known, by which shall all the mysteries and fellowships upon the earth be broken, which are not in the power of God: and now vials [Rev. 15:1, 16:21], and plagues, and thunders, and woes is coming upon the world, and the smoke of the bottomless pit hath ascended [Rev. 9:2] ... on this the Lamb's day, whose sceptre of righteousness has gone forth, who will rule the nations with a rod of iron [Rev. 12:5, 19:15], and make war in righteousness [Rev. 19:11]. There is a people come forth of the north [that is, the North of England] that shall spoil Babylon.
>
> (from Gwyn, 1986, p. 194)

Christ will come out of the quiet of the inward experience (Rev. 16:15, after Luke 12:35–40) (Gwyn, 1981, p. 74). Conflict is inevitable and necessary. Gwyn argues that Fox is clear that the true gospel can only be received by direct revelation (following Gal. 1:11–12), not by human traditions: 'When Fox proclaims that "Christ is come to teach his people himself," he is announcing that John's vision of the great battle now being waged' (1986, p. 195). Christ speaks through the obedient Quakers and directly. It is a time of reaping, of harvest, after Revelation 14:14–20. Political events in the world are seen to be signs of God's positive judgement (Gwyn, 1986, p. 197).

The true Church will re-emerge victorious out of the wilderness, the wife of Christ the Lamb (ibid.). The marriage supper of the Lamb (Rev. 21), promised in Revelation 3:20, is celebrated wherever the true Church is gathered in worship even whilst Babylon is still to be overthrown. Christ is the husband, the Church his wife (bringing an interesting interpretation of 1 Cor. 14:35, where Paul instructs the wife to be subservient to her husband in the Church) (Gwyn, 1986, p. 199). Those who dwell in this new relationship are in the New Jerusalem (see Chapter 3 below) and will witness global transformation as all is restored to a new Edenic state. In Christ, the Substance as opposed to the shadow (Heb. 10:1), early Quakers felt they stood in the fulfilment of all things (Gwyn, 1981, p. 67):

> To the extent that the Church follows the observances of the first covenant, it has lapsed back to the shadows and lost the Substance of Christian faith. To the extent that the Church observes holy days based upon pagan religions and calendars (such as Christmas), it has lost touch with both the shadows and the Substance and lives in the apostasy that has gotten up since the Apostles. The important time is the timely Day of God's intervention ... Rather than be lulled by the comforting cycle of religious holy days and seasons, the Church must be alert, never asleep to the moment of opportunity and decision.
>
> (Gwyn, 1981, pp. 90–91)

As Gwyn states, the timing of the culmination of Christ's victory is not clear (and not as clear as for whom it will come – 1981, p. 79) but what Fox emphasises time and time again is that the work has begun (John 4:23), 'Christ is come and is coming' (1986, p. 206).

This chapter considers generalised interpretations of baptism, eucharist, and the ministry as an attempt to understand Church teaching on liturgy, and in particular the eucharistic liturgy given such emphasis by most of the Church. Given this connection between the teaching of Fox and the first Friends, it explores the early Quaker response to these forms and how they claimed their own worship were more authentic and appropriate to this new and unfolding age. This chapter uses the seminal work of Douglas Gwyn (1986) and Richard Bauman (1983) extensively.

The World Council of Churches' document *Baptism, Eucharist and Ministry* (1982) lists five aspects of baptism: participation in Christ's death and resurrection; conversion, pardoning and cleansing; the gift of the Spirit; incorporation into the body of Christ, and the sign of the Kingdom:

> Baptism is the sign of new life through Jesus Christ. It unites the one baptized with Christ and with his people ... Baptism means participating in the life, death and resurrection of Jesus Christ ... by baptism, Christians are immersed in the liberating death of Christ where their sins are buried, where the 'old Adam' is crucified with Christ, and where the power of sin is broken. Thus those baptized are no longer slaves to sin, but free ... Thus those baptized are pardoned, cleansed, and sanctified by Christ ... God bestows upon all baptized persons the anointing and promise of the Holy Spirit, marks them with a seal, and implants in their hearts the first instalment of their inheritance as sons and daughters of God ... baptism is a sign and seal of ... common discipleship ... It is a sign of the Kingdom of God and of the life of the world to come.
>
> (*Baptism, Eucharist and Ministry*, 1982, pp. 2–3)

The Quaker response to the claims about water baptism rested largely in scriptural exegesis, focusing particularly on Mark 1:8: 'I indeed have baptized you with water but he shall baptize you with the Holy Ghost' (cf. John 1:33, Mat. 3:11). Thus, there was no longer a need for an outward rite: 'there is one faith which Christ Jesus is the author and finisher of; and there is one baptism, and by one spirit we are all baptized into one body' (1 Cor. 12:13), (Fox, 1990, vol. 8, p. 277). Baptism was spiritual, not outward. Gwyn suggests that the flaming sword experience of Fox in 1648, described in terms of coming through the flaming sword (see Chapter 1 above) is equated by Fox to the baptism with the Holy Spirit and with fire of Matthew 3:11, and that only those who had experienced this could experience the Paradise of God (Gwyn, 1981, p. 85).

Baptism, Eucharist and Ministry claims that the celebration of the Eucharist continues as the central act of the Church's worship (1982, p. 10). The booklet lists five aspects to the meaning of the Eucharist: as thanksgiving to the Father, as 'anamnesis' or memorial of Christ, as invocation of the Spirit, as communion of the faithful, and as meal of the Kingdom:

> In the eucharistic meal, in the eating and drinking of the bread and wine, Christ grants communion with himself. God himself acts, giving life to the body of Christ and renewing each member ... each baptized member of the body of Christ received in the eucharist the assurance of the forgiveness of sins ... the eucharist is the benediction ... by which the Church expresses its thankfulness for all God's benefits ... the eucharist is the memorial of the crucified and risen Christ ... Christ himself ... is present in this *anamnesis* ... The eucharist is also the foretaste of his parousia and of the final kingdom ... is both representation and anticipation ... the *anamnesis* of Christ is the basis and source of all Christian prayer ... the eucharistic meal is the sacrament of the body and blood of Christ, the sacrament of his real presence ... the Spirit makes the crucified and risen Christ really present ... It is in the eucharist that the community of God's people is fully manifested ... Eucharistic celebrations always have to do with the whole Church ... The eucharist opens up the vision of the divine rule which has been promised as the final renewal of creation, and is a foretaste of it.
>
> *(Baptism, Eucharist and Ministry*, 1982, pp. 10–15)

The eucharistic liturgy, probably the most common form of liturgy in the Church, is typically patterned as follows:

- hymns of praise;
- act of repentance;
- declaration of pardon;
- proclamation of the Word of God, in various forms;
- confession of faith (creed);
- intercession for the whole Church and for the world;
- preparation of the bread and wine;
- thanksgiving to the Father for the marvels of creation, redemption, and sanctification (deriving from the Jewish tradition of the *berakah*);
- the words of Christ's institution of the sacrament according to the New Testament tradition;

- the *anamnesis* or memorial of the great acts of redemption, passion, death, resurrection, ascension and Pentecost, which brought the Church into being;
- the invocation of the Holy Spirit (*epiklesis*) on the community, and the elements of bread and wine (either before the words of institution or after the memorial, or both; or some other reference to the Holy Spirit which adequately expresses the 'epiklectic' character of the eucharist);
- consecration of the faithful to God;
- reference to the communion of saints;
- prayer for the return of the Lord and the definitive manifestation of the Kingdom;
- the Amen of the whole community;
- the Lord's prayer;
- sign of reconciliation and peace;
- the breaking of the bread;
- eating and drinking in communion with Christ and with each member of the Church;
- final act of praise;
- blessing and sending. (*Baptism, Eucharist and Ministry*, 1982, pp. 15–16)

Without detailing the content of these elements of this liturgical pattern, it is clear that the focus of the service is on the remembrance of the past, and the anticipation of the future.

The meantime remembrance, thanksgiving and invocation, whilst realising important aspects of the believer's ongoing relationship with God, all hinge on past or future events. In other ways, this liturgical form takes its participants in and out of different conceptions of time. Scott Hahn emphasises that to go to Mass is to go to heaven (2003). The eucharistic prayer IV in the *Roman Missal* places the participants as united with the 'countless host of angels' standing before God (*Roman Missal*, 1975, p. 503), the prefaces explicit about the uniting of participants' voices and those of the angels. In this, it is as if the congregation is participating in the heavenly realm, operating within heavenly time. Later in the prayer, the congregation recite together how they look forward to Christ's coming in glory (*Roman Missal*, 1975, p. 506), ask God to receive those who have died into the heavenly realm, and ask God to grant to his children entrance into their 'heavenly inheritance' (*Roman Missal*, 1975, p. 507). The rite remembers the historical and that beyond history – the Second Coming (Dix, 1946, p. 264). In this sense, the participants move in and out of heaven: they participate repeatedly in a glimpse of heaven, an earnest which prefigures the full inheritance still to come:

> In the earthly liturgy we share in a foretaste of that heavenly liturgy which is celebrated in the holy city of Jerusalem toward which we journey as pilgrims, where Christ is sitting at the right hand of God, Minister of the sanctuary and of the true

tabernacle. With all the warriors of the heavenly army we sing a hymn of glory to the Lord; venerating the memory of the saints, we hope for some part and fellowship with them; we eagerly await the Saviour, our Lord Jesus Christ, until He, our life, shall appear and we too will appear with Him in glory.

(Hahn, 2003, p. 11)

The community which is collected together and renewed through the rite grounds its identity as a people collected in the past, given the earnest of what is to come, and who anticipate the Second Coming. Only the cycle of sanctification, sinning and repentance are thoroughly present tense.

At the same time, the intimacy of the Mass should not be underplayed: 'The Church believes that the Lord Jesus is really present among us in a wonderful way under the eucharistic species' (*Roman Missal*, 1975, xiv): 'As I saw the priest raise that white host, I felt a prayer surge from my heart in a whisper: "My Lord and my God. That's really you!" ' (Hahn, 2003, p. 8).

Early Friends did not use this dimension of temporary-ness as a criticism of outward communion. Rather they turned on its artificiality, outwardness and redundancy. Graves quotes an early Quaker preacher comparing the outward, and therefore carnal, communion with an effective inward communion: 'Life flows from Vessel to Vessel, and here a Communion, indeed not a communion of Bread and Wine, as the World Receives, which is carnal; their Wine satisfies not the Soul, it washest not from Sin, nor cleanseth from Transgression' (Graves, 1972, p. 162). In the case of communion, the first Quakers do not dispute the scriptural injunction (as they would do later – see Chapters 3 and 4):

For I have received of the Lord that which also I delivered unto you, That the Lord Jesus the same night in which he was betrayed took bread: And when he had given thanks, he brake it, and said, Take, eat: this is my body, which is broken for you: this do in remembrance of me. After the same manner also he took the cup, when he had supped, saying, This cup is the new testament in my blood: this do ye, as oft as ye drink it, in remembrance of me. For as often as ye eat this bread, and drink this cup, ye do shew the Lord's death till he come.

(1 Cor. 11:23–6)

Neither do they appear to criticise the connection made between this passage and those in John 6 as they would do later:

For the bread of God is he which cometh down from heaven, and giveth life unto the world ... And Jesus said unto them, I am the bread of life: he that cometh to me shall never hunger: and he that believeth on me shall never thirst. (John 6:33, 35)

Then Jesus said unto them, Verily, verily I say unto you, Except ye eat the flesh of the Son of man, and drink his blood, ye have no life in you. Whoso eateth my flesh, and drinketh my blood, hath eternal life; and I will raise him up at the last day ... He that eateth my flesh my flesh, and drinketh my blood, dwelleth in me, and I in him. As the living Father hath sent me, and I live by the Father: so he that eateth me, even he shall live by me. This is that bread which came down from heaven: not as your fathers did eat manna and are dead; he that eateth of this bread shall live for ever.

(John 6:53–4, 56–8)

In his 1685 leaflet, *A Distinction Between the Two Suppers* (1991), Fox makes it clear that the injunction to break the bread in remembrance of the death of Christ, qualified by the phrase 'till he come' (1 Cor. 11:26), is fulfilled within the Book of Luke (24:35): 'If he be witnessed within, and known within, then he is come, then what need you have bread and wine to put you in remembrance of him?' (Fox, 1990, vol. 4, p. 237).

Rather, the passage from Revelation 3:20 ('Behold, I stand at the door and knock: if any man hear my voice, and open the door, I will come into him, and will sup with him, and he with me'), given to the Church through the Apostle John, is the more appropriate instruction: 'They who do not hear the spiritual voice of Christ, when he stands at the door and knocks, are such as err from the Spirit of God, and Faith of Christ, and hate his Light and go from the Grace and Truth in their hearts' (*A Distinction Between the Two Suppers*, 1991, p. 9). In other words, other Christians are focusing on the wrong supper. Fox continues that only true Christians are called to the marriage supper of the Lamb, the second and real 'Last Supper'. Those partaking in the other supper are denying the coming of Christ and are involved in an anachronistic rite.

In other words, as with worship itself, the outward form is only a continuation of the individual experience, an intentional collective sacramentality as opposed to the continual personal one. In his audience with Pope Alexander VII in 1658, the Quaker John Luffe claimed 'every day is a Sabbath wherein we can serve God.' The Pope asked if there was then nothing to be done 'for the remembrance sake of our Saviour's blessed ascension'. 'No, no,' replied Luffe, 'I have Christ about me and in me and cannot choose but remember Him continually' (Braithwaite, 1912, p. 424).

In Luffe's case, Christ's presence was continual and embodied apart from the eucharistic rite. At the same time, the sacrifice of Christ as a liturgical theme was replaced by the victory of Christ and the establishment of heaven on earth. Again, we find the inward/outward dichotomy: 'So now people are … to be brought from their outward Crosses to the Cross of Christ, the power of God within them … Then the outward, dead crosses of Stone, Wood, Silver or Gold they shall not need to put them in Remembrance of Christ, or to bring him into their minds' (Fox, 1990, vol. 7, p. 103).

Stephen Crisp, in a 1688 sermon, was explicit about an inward communion:

> Christ the Mediator, stands at the door and knocks; He will come in and sup with thee; if thou openest to Him; then we shall meet with the Lord's Supper: *This is the Lord, I will wait for him*; He will bring his bread with Him, the Bread of Life, and the Wine of his kingdom; and the Lord's Supper will be celebrated without cavilling and jangling.
>
> (Tuke, 1824, p. 432)

Early Quakers found their communion realised inwardly, and understood it as the communion with Christ foretold in Revelation, not the one instructed by Corinthians which was now superseded.

Quakers were also particularly critical of the separated ministry. First, the clergy preached an anachronistic way that held the people back from the new experience now available to them. Second, they were paid for the word of God that was free. Third, they themselves were unnecessary, a symbol of apostasy and stratification. On this last point, Dewsbury wrote:

> God alone is the teacher of his people, and hath given to everyone a measure of Grace, that checks and reproves sin, in the secrets of the heart and conscience; and all that wait in the light, which comes from Christ for the power of Jesus Christ to destroy sin, and to guide them in obedience to the light, so that they come to know the only true God and father of light in Christ Jesus, who is the way to him ... I came to the knowledge of eternal life, not by the letter of the scriptures, nor hearing men speak of the name of God [but] by the inspiration of the spirit of Jesus Christ, the lion of the tribe of Judah.
>
> (Dewsbury, 1689, p. 54)

In a sense, Quakers were preaching a collective ordination as a set-apart group, bestowed with authority by God to help build up the community and fulfil its calling. Collectively, the faithful were the Church, not any building (Bauman, 1983, p. 64):

> Upon meeting we sit silent in the tongue, yet having a heart full of praise, where we worship God in Spirit and truth [after John 4:23–24], who makes our bodies temples for the same Spirit: not speaking by hearsay and humane Arts, but lay all that down; when earthly thoughts, earthly words, and earthly works are all laid aside, and the temple within us is ready, the light of Christ shining in it; and the Lord with a further manifestation of his love enters it by his clerical power; where upon we can truly say, that the Lord's presence is amongst us, feeding of the Flock, and making us feel the power of an endless life.
>
> (Britten, 1660, p. 2)

Today, the Church talks of the 'royal and prophetic priesthood of all baptized' (*Baptism, Eucharist and Ministry*, 1982, p. 23), a ministry of intercession, as well as the priesthood of Christ, a ministry of sacrifice. For early Friends, this priesthood of Christ was not mediated, but Christ himself was the high priest. Fox talks of the end of the old priesthood and a new everlasting priesthood of which Christ is the high priest (1891, vol. 1, pp. 355–6). To ignore this new reality would be an offence against Jesus Christ (*A Distinction Between the Two Suppers*, 1991, p. 2).

The apostolic succession was not to pass through the Vicar of Rome, or through Scripture and the priestly rule of expertise, but through the whole people of God.

The passages from Matthew 12:48, and Mark 3:33 ('who shall do the will of God, these, are my brethren') reinforce this point:

> And those that are come to the pure silence of the flesh, to bridle the tongue, to wrestle with the spiritual wickedness in high places of the heart, that each thought may be brought into obedience unto Christ, and whatsoever they act, do all to the glory of God, such can witness the power of Christ in them and when he pleases to call them by his eternal Spirit to go forth as Ministers, they can best declare what God hath revealed unto them.
>
> (Britten, 1660, p. 11)

Quaker revelation mirrored the insights of early Christianity: the immediacy of direct knowledge of God experienced in the last days meant that 'the delimitation of sacred space reserved for special priesthood, and requiring special priestly acts which only some can perform' was no longer appropriate: 'what had required the mediation of priest previously was now open to all through the direct mediation of Christ' (Dunn, 1991, p. 92). Ministers were any called by the inward power, 'and being by the same in measure purified and sanctified, he comes thereby to be called and moved to minister to others, being able to speak from a living experience of what he himself is a witness' (Barclay, 2002, p. 237).

The Quaker attitude to time, the realisation of intimacy and of baptism by, and communion with, God, and the redundancy of a separated ministry, led inherently to a flat ecclesiology, a level church. This combined with the idea of a free ministry legitimated a worship form based in silence:

> Through the liturgical drama, the participants are taken into the story. There they not only re-present it, but their identity is shaped by it, and their lives (history, present and future) are read into the story, which is now claimed as their own. To a significant degree, this community's remembering of its own story depends upon (perhaps even, is contingent upon) the liturgical ... reenactment of it.
>
> (Johns, 1998, p. 35)

The first Quakers may have been consciously re-enacting the half hour of silence in heaven following the opening of the seventh seal (Rev. 8:1). In an Epistle, Fox chides the world's ignorance for not knowing the time to keep silent and the time to speak (Eccles. 3:7) and continues, initially with reference to Ezekiel: 'He that hath an ear to hear, let him hear: such as know the seven seals, shall know the silence in heaven. And when I saw the seven seals, there was silence for half an hour in heaven; he that can, read this, and understand' (Fox, 1990, Vol. 4, p. 119).

Bauman makes the additional point that the early Quakers were wary of 'carnal talk' and of 'fleshly speaking', of 'idle words' after Matthew 12:36: 'At the foundation of these principles was the powerfully resonant awareness that natural languages came into being at Babel and that only by regaining the "state Adam was

in before he fell" could one comprehend the eternal and "divine word of wisdom" '
(1983, p. 21).

As Hahn (2003) suggests of Mass, worship takes participants to heaven. Or
rather, in the Quaker case, the establishment of heaven on earth was reflected in the
worship experience. For Fox, the participants were those given the invitation to this
transformation.

Silence-based worship was perhaps borrowed from the Seekers who had already
stripped away much that was outward or deemed apostate (Gwyn, 1986, p. 153). It
was perhaps underpinned by the quotation from Revelation about silence in heaven,
(or Zeph. 1:7 which tells us to keep silent for the Day of the Lord is at hand, or 'let
your words be few' from Eccles. 5:2). For whatever reason(s), Quakers adopted this
form for their public worship (different from the threshing meetings where Quaker
ministers would argue ideas with their opponents). It was radical and it reflected the
experience and the mission of the early Quaker movement.

Gwyn argues that the early Quaker message stood apart from renewal and reform
and therefore the existing Protestant and Roman Catholic structures: 'It was their
calling to raze the structures of the churches to their foundations and to *restore* men
and women upon the foundation of Christ's teaching' (Gwyn, 1986, p. 179).
Bauman concurs: where Protestantism had interiorised much ritual, Quakers took it
a step further with their interiorisation of the Word, and in their shift of emphasis
from outward verbal preaching to letting the life preach (1983, p. 30). Even where
outward speech as used, it was in terms of a silencing of self and will. Certainly the
form of worship maintained a clear contrast with the worldly outward forms of the
apostate Church.

The purpose of worship was not to sustain the faithful in the meantime but to
help those in the vanguard of the endtime remain obedient, to hear God through
Christ directly. It was a worship to supersede all previous forms of worship, and a
worship to end the confusion and schism endemic to the 1640s (Gwyn, 1986,
p. 156):

> Now, thou must die in the silence, to the fleshly wisdom, knowledge, reason, and
> understanding ... Keep to that of God in you which will lead you up to God, when
> you are still from your own thoughts, and imaginations, and desires and counsels of
> your own hearts, and motions, and will; when you stand single from all these, waiting
> upon the Lord, your strength is renewed.
>
> (Fox, 1990, vol. 4, p. 132)

Moreover, such worship was the means to the endtime. Dying to one's self in the
silence and being reborn was proto-eschatological, a personal endtime that
necessarily prefigured global transformation. Gwyn outlines Fox's fluent use of
Scripture in urging watchful and silent waiting (Pss. 25, 27, 37; Eccles. 3:7; Zech.
2:13; Matt. 25:13; James 5:8; 1 Pet. 4:7; also Hab. 2:20; Zeph. 1:7; 1 Cor. 14:28,
30, 34, and Eph. 19:1), and states 'waiting upon the Lord, stopping one's self, is the

taking up of the cross in worship' (1986, p. 161). In these terms, the experience of the silence offered direct knowledge of what was to come for the whole world. It was similar to Paul's experience except that this time it was not to be limited to only certain individuals.

Silence was about both the stopping of that which needed to be silenced (Bauman, 1983, p. 22), as well as a reverential and unencumbered state for the encounter with Christ. It was both a closing-down of the old life and an opening-up to God's Word and the new life. It was both a consequence of experience and a means to it, both experiential and educative. Ultimately then it was apocalyptic, concerned with the revelation of the endtime (Gwyn, 1986, p. 158).

Ideally, worship could be held wholly in silence with great effectiveness. The Welsh Quaker Richard Davies wrote:

> Though it was silent from words, yet the word of the Lord God was among us; it was as a hammer and a fire; it was sharper than any two-edged sword; it pierced through our inward parts; it melted and brought us into tears that there was scarcely a dry eye among us. The Lord's blessed power overshadowed our meeting, and I could have said that God alone was master of that assembly.
>
> (Kirk, 1978, p. 91)

The purpose of speech, vocal ministry, then, was to only bring people further into this inward experience. As Bauman states:

> That is, silence, and especially the silent communion of worshippers, is the most desirable spiritual state for the conduct of collective worship. Any speaking that should take place during worship must emerge from the inward silence of the speaker and be directed toward bringing the auditors to silence or enhancing the condition of silence in which they already reside.
>
> (1983, p. 125)

Bauman summates, 'Silence is both antecedent to speaking in worship and the end of speaking in worship; silence precedes speaking, is the ground of speaking, and is the consequence of speaking' (1983, p. 126). Silence coming from dependence on God would prepare participants to minister vocally if led to by God, and to receive within that framework of dependence and obedience. Bauman suggests the possibility that the first years of Quaker Meetings were mainly silent, as if there was a chronology of a preparatory period of silent gathering prior to the faithful being given outward words to speak and to hear (1983, pp. 125–6).

Given the desire to die to the self in worship and avoid will-worship, the speaker was defined as entirely passive, merely a channel for the Word of God (Ezek. 3:27, 33:22; Matt. 10:20): 'And as the bodies of men and women subjected unto and guided by the spirit of God are the temple of God; therefore the Spirit of God may speak in and through them; and as the Lord is the teacher of his people he may be the speaker in them and through them' (Farnsworth, 1663, cited in Bauman, 1983,

p. 25). In time, a distinct nasal tone would be adopted to differentiate the human's voice from the ministry passing through her or him (see Chapter 3).

Bauman identifies two forms of vocal contribution: prayer and preaching. In prayer, the speaker would kneel and the rest of the Meeting stand and remove their hats, an honour they reserved for God alone (1983, p. 128). Preaching, the speaker would stand, the rest remain seated. Contributions would be weighed in the silence in much the way Paul suggests in 1 Corinthians 14. Meetings, often three hours long, and sometimes longer, might include long periods of silence or be totally free of speech.

Both Bauman and Gwyn recognise the problems inherent in the free ministry and the need for some form of control against, for example, contributions that did not arise from the right place, forms of speech that strayed from the spiritual path in their artistry ('high words') or were errant in their timing or length. Bauman gives the example of John Stubbs who confessed to Margaret Fell of being unfaithful in his vocal ministry: 'I never fell into more disobedience than last meeting at thy house, and was warned of it before, for, when the spring and well was set open, but then I did not speak, but in the dread I spoke, but the life was shut up, and I felt it to my condemnation' (1983, p. 131). In other words, Stubbs had not ministered when he had been prompted but then, feeling his lack of obedience, had ministered later without divine prompting, consequently feeling convicted of this shortcoming.

Given the power of silence, speaking was a risky business and could only be validated as authentic by how it had 'reached' people after the fact. At the same time, hesitation to speak was also a shortcoming, betraying a lack of passivity and obedience. Those recognised as 'Ministers', that is, being perceived to have a gift of ministry, were those most likely to speak, and thus, those most likely to wrestle with working out what was truly from God, when it should be shared, and whether they could be capable in their sharing of it, a process which could be extended (Bauman, 1983, pp. 132–6):

> After many years travail of spirit ... in the year 1670, and the thirty third year of my age, God almighty raised me up by his power, which had been working in my heart many years, to preach the everlasting gospel of life and salvation; and then a fresh exercise began: for the enemy tempted me to withstand the Lord, to look to my own weakness of body and spirit, and insufficiency for such a great work ... For when the power of God fell upon me, and a few words were required of me to speak in the assemblies of the Lord's people in Bristol, I reasoned they were a wise people, and how could it be that I should add to them; also, that I might hurt myself; that imagination might be the ground of such requirings, and that many wise men therein might look upon me as forward, and so judge me; and thus I reasoned through some meetings until I was in sore distress. When those meetings were over, wherein I had been disobedient, then great was my burden. Oh, then was I ready to engage and covenant with the Lord, that if I felt the requirings of his power again, I would faithfully give up in obedience unto him. Yet when I was tried again, the same rebellious mind would be stirred by the power of the enemy; then hath the Lord withdrawn the motions and the feeling of his power, and all refreshment with it, and

hid his face ... And when I began [again] to feel the warming power of God stirring in my inward man, I was glad on one hand, but very sorrowful on the other, fearing lest I should be rebellious again: and so hard was it for me to open my mouth in those meetings at Bristol, that had the Lord not caused his power so to be manifest in my heart, as new wine in a vessel that wanted vent, I might have perished.

(Charles Marshall, in Bauman, 1983, pp. 133–4)

Negative judgements of ministry were common but discouraged, any disciplining except in extreme circumstances left until after the Meeting (Bauman, 1983, p. 135). A fuller consideration of the ways in which the silence is managed today is given in Chapter 6.

In the twentieth century, Otto had this to say about Quaker silence:

Such impressive moments of silence ... are the culminating sacramental point in the worship, denoting as they do the instant when 'God is in the midst' ... what was previously only possessed in insufficiency, only longed for, now comes upon the scene in living actuality, the experience of the transcendent in gracious intimate presence, the Lord's Visitation of His people. Such a realization is Sacrament ... such a silence is therefore a sacramental silence ... Worship of the Quakers is in fact a realization of Communion in both senses of the word – inward oneness and fellowship of the individual with the invisible present Reality and the mystical union of many individuals with one another. In this regard there is the plainest inward kinship between ... the Quaker meeting and the Roman Catholic Mass. *Both* are solemn religious observances of a numinous and sacramental character, *both* are communion, both exhibit alike an inner straining not only to 'realize the presence' of God, but to attain a degree of oneness with him.

(1923, pp. 217–18)

At one level, Otto is correct. However, as these last two chapters have shown, early Quakers and Roman Catholics were starting from very different places their understanding of their place in biblical time. For Friends, this was founded in an intimacy with God involving unmediated access and a sense of being set free from sin. It was expressed in and through silent worship, a silence of curtailment and a silence of new possibility in clear distinction to anachronistic liturgical forms that focused on earlier modes of relationship with God and Christ. Speaking was only to bring people into the silence, to quake in expectation, and to allow the Word to be heard through the passive vessel of the obedient servant. The free ministry was risky and there was plenty of advice as to how best guard against its dangers. Otto's reference to 'straining' doesn't accord with the early Quaker journals and the emphasis on mystical union as an aim seems implicit in those texts. What the journals reveal instead, particularly amongst those who spoke in Meeting the most, was the continual struggle to discern what might be the obedient path. This personal struggle was to come to typify the whole movement as we shall see in the next chapter.

CHAPTER 3

In the World But Not of It

Thomas Ellwood's experience of convincement and the intimacy that accompanied it took place during worship:

> This latter meeting was like the clinching of a nail confirming and fastening in my mind those good principles which had sunk into me at the former ... and now I saw that ... the spirit of the world had hitherto ruled in me, and led me into pride, flattery, vanity, and superfluity, all of which was naught. Now was all my former life ripped up, and my sins by degrees were set in order before me ... I found that all sin brought guilt ... This I felt, and was greatly bowed down under the sense thereof. Now also did I receive a new law ... the law of the spirit in Christ Jesus, which was wrought in me against all evil ... so that every thing was brought to judgement ... Thus the Lord was graciously pleased to dwell in me ... I was now required by the inward and spiritual law ... to put away the evil of my doings, and to cease to do evil ...
>
> (Ellwood, 1885, p. 29)

The covenant required a change of approach, an end to the inclination to sin:

> The strength of my god appeared in me so was I made perfect, through weakness ... With his love he doth embrace me ... he fills me with sweet smelling savours, perfumed with heavenly odors ... he waters me with heavenly dews ... he hath fashioned me according to his will, a vessel fit to put in what he will; I am not mine but the lords.
>
> (Samuel Hooton, n.d, in Mack, 1992, p. 163)

This idea of being a vessel for God in worship and in life generally is amplified in accounts that suggest that the transformation of these first Friends through their convincement involved being taken into a place separate from the rest of humanity. That is, that the consequent intimacy with God placed these Friends in a different relationship of knowing and being known than other humans. This chapter considers the degree to which these Friends found themselves out of 'the world' before looking at how the sense of time, intimacy, and separation changed between the seventeenth and eighteenth centuries.

Coleman and Collins have used Bourdieu's concept of 'habitus' as a theoretical framework within which to interpret Liberal Quakerism. This idea of habitus refers to a cultural and embodied homogeneity to personal and collective social life, a coherence to life which is not context-specific but which is regulated by inherent dispositions (Coleman and Collins, 2000, p. 318). Distinctions between sacred and profane, for example, break down: 'practices of collective and individual worship can become techniques of the body and embodied dispositions that cannot simply be shut off, once the believer leaves a service' (Coleman and Collins, 2000, p. 318). While Coleman and Collins' claims for a present-day Liberal Quaker habitus (2000) appear to me questionable, the idea that worship and the rest of life were part of the same social fabric for early Friends seems to be likely, given the accounts which survive. However, it seems also clear that this extended sacred state could draw up new distinctions with the profane.

As mentioned in Chapter 2, the relationship between early Quaker teaching and the book of Revelation brought with it New Jerusalem imagery. Gwyn quotes the following from Fox:

> I saw the state of the city New Jerusalem, which comes out of heaven ... which the professors had looked upon to be like an outward city or some town that had come out of the elements ... The spiritual reign of Christ Jesus in this great city ... is within the light, the city of the living God ... so here is the city within the light [where] there is no place or language, but there his voice may be heard. The gate stands open night and day that all may come in here ... Without the city are dogs [Rev. 22:15] ... within this city, here is light, here is life, here is the heavenly bread and blood of the Lamb to eat and drink of ... I am just in the city. Oh the heavenly Jerusalem, the bride is come down, the marriage of the lamb that must go over all the false cities that have gotten up since the apostles' days ... This true city is come down since the apostles' days and is coming down from God ... All that are within the light of Christ and his faith ... and within the Spirit and the Holy Ghost that Christ and the apostles and prophets were in ... all that come to this heavenly city, New Jerusalem, that is above the old [and] which is the mother of all true Christians ... must come to the truth and light in their hearts ... if they come to be members of this city ... and so grafted into [Christ Jesus (see Rom. 11:17–24)] that they might bring forth heavenly fruit to the heavenly Father that has begotten them and drawn them unto Christ.
> (Fox, 1911, Vol. 1, pp. 170–174, in Gwyn, 1986, pp. 199–200)

This is an account of a vision. However, at times, it seems that some early Friends really felt themselves somewhere else, in a separated space whilst still operating in this world. In his tract, *The Trumpet of the Lord Sounded Forth Out of Zion*, Edward Burrough is clear of a separation between how he is known by 'the world' and who he really is. The authorship is attributed to 'one whose name is truly known by the children of the same birth, but unknown to the world, though by it called Edward Burrough' (Burrough, 1656, cover). Further into the tract, in a piece addressed to other Quakers, Burrough writes:

> To all you who are in the light of eternal life, which doth comprehend the world, who are born from above, of the immortal word which doth live for ever, who are not of the world ... who are not known to the world (though by it scornfully called Quakers) even you doth the Lord also remember with everlasting kindness, and infinite love, of whose beginning and End there is none, and whose height, depth, measure and limit cannot be found out; for you hath he chosen above all the Families of the Earth, to place his Name among, and to establish his everlasting Covenant ...
> (Burrough, 1656, p. 33)

Burrough is suggesting that Quakers are those 'born from above' and 'not of the world'. Such sentiment resonates with the following passage from Revelation: 'Him that overcometh will I make a pillar in the temple of my God, and he shall go no more out: and I will write upon him the name of my God, and the name of the city of my God, which is new Jerusalem, which cometh down out of heaven from my God: and I will write upon him my new name' (Rev. 3:12).

There is also the passage from Isaiah 65:15 where it is prophesied that God will 'call his servants by another name'. The following excerpt is from a letter written from Fox to Oliver Cromwell prior to their meeting in 1654:

> I (who am of the world called George ffox) doe deny the carrying or drawing of any carnall sword against any, or against thee Oliver Crumwell or any man in the presence of the lord god I declare it (God is my wittnesse, by whom I am moved to give this forth for truthes sake, from him whom the world called George ffox who is the son of God) and who is sent to stand A witnesse against all violence ... my kingdom is not of this world, therefore with Carnal weapons I do not fight. [signed] Ff. G. who is of the world called George ffox who A new name hath which the world knowes not. Wee are wittnesses of this testimony. (whose names in the flesh is Thomas Aldam. Robert Creven)
>
> (Fox, 1911, pp. 161–2)

The duality of 'the world' and of God's kingdom is clear. Friends were known by their outward worldly names in the world but truly only known, and known by their new name, by God. Bauman gives examples of Friends' accounts in which they could not speak or understand the language of those they conversed with but where they nevertheless believed the Truth could be communicated (1983, p. 27). Again, the outward is insignificant contrasted with a higher inward state.

Gay Pilgrim has described this Quaker sense of alternate ordering in terms of Foucault's (and Hetherington's) use of the term 'heterotopia' (Pilgrim, 2004). By this, she means the way in which Quakers set up alternative discourses/spaces that led to dissonance between themselves and the world they inhabited. She uses the example of the courtroom and the Quaker refusal to swear or recognise the authority of the court as one way in which Quakers shifted the location and meaning of discourse and interaction. Another heterotopic space created by Friends were their prison cells. Fox 'turned the site of his imprisonment into a site of Otherness; a space which he used to evangelise and inspire, contrary to the intention that it should humiliate and defeat him' (Pilgrim, 2004, p. 211). 'Doing time' became transposed onto a different temporal and spiritual plane. Meeting for Worship itself reflected this sense of alternate ordering (Pilgrim, 2004, p. 212), given how different the practice was from other churches and in not-speaking, how different from 'the world'.

What isn't clear to scholars is the degree to which this dualism towards the world pointed to a real or metaphysical union with God or the extent to which an alternate physical ordering took Friends beyond the physical, beyond the material in their own self-conceptions, that is, that they were in their bodies but not of them. These ideas are discussed further below: what we can say is that the outward in the Barclayan sense was deemed secondary, epistemologically inferior (Creasey 1962, p. 12). Of Richard Hubberthorne, Sarah Blackborrow wrote: 'His mind was redeemed out of visible things' (Blackborrow, 1663, (a)3r): 'As there can be nothing more opposite to the natural will and wisdom of man than this silent waiting upon God, so neither can it be obtained nor rightly comprehended by man but as he layeth down his own wisdom and will so as to be content to be thoroughly subject to God' (Barclay, 2002, p. 297).

Quakers depict themselves as un-natural, non-worldly, and inhabiting a space centred on God and the inward, rather than the outwardly and creaturely. Fox's dying words included: 'I am glad I was here ...' (Fox, 1891, vol. 2., p. 505) suggesting a dualistic attitude between 'here' and 'I'. As Burrough wrote:

> While waiting upon the Lord in silence, as often as we did for many hours together, with our minds and hearts towards him, being stayed in the light of Christ within us from all thoughts, fleshly motions and desires, we received often the pouring down of the spirit upon us, and our hearts were made glad and our tongues loosened, and our mouths opened, and we spake with new tongues, as the Lord gave us utterance, and his spirit led us, which was poured upon us, as sons and daughters, and to us hereby was the deep things of God revealed, and things unutterable was known and made manifest.
>
> (Fox 1659, prelim. leaves b1–b2)

In this Quaker pentecost experience, Quakers are remodelled and given new tongues. Bauman notes that Friends were charged with a distinctive style of speaking: 'his religion is, not to speak like his neighbours' and, from the same critic, 'his religion is nothing but phrases, being a superstitious observer of new-minted modes of speaking' (1983, p. 8). At the same time, Quakers devalued speech (Bauman, 1983, p. 10).

Phyllis Mack characterises Friends as a people 'whose aim was to transcend the limitations of their outward circumstances' (Mack, 1992, p. 141):

> ... both will and mind were, quite simply, the enemies of the soul, and the first object of Quaker meditation, prayer, good deeds, or visions was to suffocate impulses towards personal expression and achieve the annihilation of the thinking self ... 'See your thoughts and deny them,' declared Priscilla Cotton.
>
> (Mack, 1992, p. 142)

Bauman suggests that speaking itself out of the wrong source could be denounced as worldly (1983, p. 21). Silence was a more appropriate vehicle for spiritual attainment: 'silence, as the cessation of outward speaking, became a metaphor for the suppresion of all joining to the flesh' and of the personal sacrifice corresponding to the cross, hence the use of Ecclesiates 5:2, 'let your words be few' (Bauman, 1983, p. 22). Silence, was, of course, not passive or necessarily static. Work by

Mack (1992) and Tarter (1993) on Quaker women highlights the physicality of the worship experience.

Mack argues that the very physical expression of their spirituality not only denoted its intensity but also expressed the irrelevance of intelligence and common sense (1992, p. 151). On one occasion, they persuaded a Dutch minister against using a translator – in Mack's words, 'they knew well that the prophet's deeper message was nonsense; literally non-sense' (1992, p. 143). Mack argues that Friends transcended gender, self, and even adulthood, in their self-expression. All were brides of Christ and children of God, subservient before God but raised above the world and their individual states (1992, pp. 236–7). At other times adopting male patterns of expression, all Quakers balanced multiple identities and roles within the movement.

In Richard Bailey's work on George Fox, he argues that early Friends experienced 'celestial inhabitation'. The Quaker experience was not simply about Christocentricism but Christopresentism, a divinisation through the possession of the believer by Christ's flesh and bone (Bailey, 1992). This inward state led to outward manifestations of perfection, continuous ecstasy and exalted language.

Bailey concurs with other scholarship, such as Gwyn's in tying Fox's prophecy to a biblical sense of history in which the book of Revelation was key in understanding what was taking place in the 1650s. However, Bailey goes further than other scholars in suggesting that Fox felt himself personally central to the ending of 1600 years of apostasy. Fox himself was the prophet or messenger of God to call the world finally and for all time back from the Satanic delusion of outward religion, the religion of the Beast: 'If Fox democratized the potential for divine sonship he reserved for himself the pre-eminent status of avatar – a special manifestation of the divine in the last days' (Bailey, 1992, p. 115).

Christ in Fox spoke the message, connecting with the Seed of God (Christ) which dwelt in all; 'the Kingdom grew from the inside out' (Bailey, 1992, p. 37). Bailey also suggests that in the Quaker instance, this kind of theology, itself common in seventeenth-century England, was informed and shaped by Christopresentism: 'the literal incarnation of the flesh and bone of the Glorified Christ (indeed of the whole Godhead) within the believer made the notion of realized eschatology intensely personal' (ibid., p. 39).

In *The Great Mystery of the Great Whore Unfolded*, Fox offers the following: 'God's Christ is not distinct from his saints, nor their bodies, for he is within them; nor distinct from their spirits, for their spirits witness him ... he is in the saints, and they eat his flesh, and sit with him in heavenly places' (Fox, 1990, vol. 3, p. 340). The Lord's Supper is inward and continuous.

> With Fox, more than Grace is infused into the believer. The inhabitation of the celestial Christ within effects a pervasive and permanent transformation wherein the saint is divinized. Perhaps the notion of the permanent transubstantiation of the believer into Christ – so the believer becomes the sacrament – is closer to the mark if

we use the terms 'transference' or 'transposition'. Whatever, Fox's inner Christ was a celestial (not a 'spiritual') Christ with an immaterial 'flesh and bone'.

(Bailey, 1992, p. 79)

It was not that Fox thought himself as Christ, but that he was inhabited by Christ. Outwardly, he was Fox. Inwardly he was inhabited by Christ (Bailey, 1992, p. 88). Thus, Bailey argues, 'when Fox spoke he spoke not as George Fox but as Christ' (1992, p. 89). The outward body is merely a garment for the divine: 'Fox's interpretation of the Biblical phrase "flesh of my flesh" was quite literal ... Quakers were literally transformed into heavenly beings, that is, although the forms of their bodies did not change their inner beings were qualitatively deified' (Bailey, 1992, p. 96).

Tried for blasphemy on the charge that he thought himself equal to God, Fox answered instead in terms of unity, implying that equality could only be possible between distinct entities (Bailey, 1992, p. 104). A second line of defence was to distinguish between the earthly creature, and the Christ within (ibid.), between how he was known by the world and how he was known by God (Fox, 1911, pp. 161–2). Bailey argues that when Fox answered to accusers that he was the Son of God and had seen the face of God, he was answering as the Christ who inhabited him and spoke through him (Bailey, 1992, p. 111).

Where scholars disagree is the extent to which the inward Second Coming of Christ is a literal physical manifestation, and the degree to which the Light of Christ is inward, that is, coming in from outside, or inner. Partly it is a matter of the interpretation of Quaker text, partly a difficulty with the lack of consistency between Quaker writers and even within the work of Fox himself. Bailey himself suggests that early Quaker Christology was not homogeneous (2004), even before it was prone to later modification by second-generation converts such as Penn and Barclay (Bailey, 1992, pp. 227–41). These later thinkers downplayed the physicality of the inward Christ and the 'not distinct' language of the passage above from Fox, claiming instead that reason and conscience were the vehicle for God's transformation of humanity.

Of the scholars who agree with the general direction of Bailey's ideas, Michele Tarter takes up the idea of celestial inhabitation in her analysis of an embodied Quaker spirituality, whereas Glen Reynolds argues that Bailey is too literal in his interpretation of Fox and that the union with Christ is metaphysical. These scholars are considered briefly in turn.

Tarter's focus is on the role of the body in Quaker worship. She writes: 'the act of quaking was an act laden with meaning and purpose: it was the motion of spiritual rebirth and apocalyptic delivery' (Tarter, 2001, p. 147). Here, the scriptural precedent is provided by Joel:

And it shall come to pass afterward, that I will pour out my spirit upon all flesh; and your sons and your daughters shall prophesy, your old men shall dream dreams, your young men shall see visions: and also upon the servants and upon the handmaids in those days will I pour out my spirit.

(Joel 2:28–9)

Whereas Gwyn takes this less literally (1986, p. 157), Tarter uses this text and the Quaker use of it to support Bailey's ideas of Christopresentism:

> In his theology of Christopresentism, the leader [George Fox] declared that when spirit poured onto flesh, Friends returned to a prelapsarian state and experienced a concrete, substantial, and visceral convincement; indeed, they 'magnified' the 'indwelling Christ' and embodied perfection on earth. Such a proclamation rejected the limitations of dualism, celebrating the fusion of flesh and spirit for all humankind. In this corporeal manifestation of God, a worshipper became 'celestial flesh' ...
>
> (Tarter, 2001, p. 148)

For Tarter, quaking signified the very coming of Christ: 'salvation came not despite the body but rather because of it'; 'Ridding religious worship of all icons and sacraments, including the rite of communion, the Friends perceived themselves as living texts of Christianity, the celestial flesh of a millennial world' (Tarter, 2001, pp. 148–9).

Tarter argues that this embodied theology was particularly poignant for women who often 'suffered severely for being framed as the trope of body and nature'. Instead of being categorised as weaker, women Friends were affirmed as at least spiritually equal to men and were empowered by the associations linking their bodies with the body of Christ. She claims that women more than men manifested the divine currents running through their bodies, often swooning, writhing on the floor, and howling as if in childbirth, finally roaring louder than any man (Tarter, 2001, p. 149). She argues that worship became a ' "feminine" space – volatile, permeable, and free', destabilising patriarchal modes of liturgical performance: 'Silence in the Friends' meetings privileged the language of the body, allowing the "indwelling Christ" to move forth in dynamic, performative agency' (ibid., p. 150).

This idea of performance was not lost on the anti-Quakers. The spectacle of Quaking, sometimes sexualised by puritan critics as a way of secularising the experience and casting the women in particular as deviant, was attacked as seductive, dangerous to the onlooker as any theatre would be. At other times, cast as theatre, Quaking was compared with Papish high rite (Tarter, 2001, p. 151).

What was taken by Friends as beyond the world, out of the material, was cast as carnal and worldly. Friends were clear that the external and the worldly were dangerous and corrupt categories: 'See if ye do not find something in your understandings made manifest which is Eternal to guide your minds out of all External things, which wither away and fade' (Fox, 1990, vol. 7, p. 26). Similarly, the teenager James Parnell wrote to his convert, Stephen Crisp:

Therefore be still in the measure of light which exerciseth thy mind unto God, and *will* nothing; but let thoughts be judged, and the power of God work, that He may be seen to all. And by this alone principle thou mayest be led and acted forth in the cross unto the carnal, and the denial of self, in particular and in general ...

(Tuke, 1824, p. 3)

For Glen Reynolds, the divinisation or deification process is metaphysical rather than embodied. Rather than make the flesh divine, Reynolds argues that Fox was talking about deification through the reunion of the soul with God. In other words, rather than filling the body with Christ in a corporeal sense, the Light of Christ and the soul were united in a metaphysical union. Unique amongst scholars of Quakerism, Reynolds claims this process is realisable on earth but is not complete until after death, thus denying the possibility of full perfection of humanity and eschatological completion on earth. 'Flesh and bone' language, for Reynolds, is allegorical of a more individualised process of union and eschatological completion completed after death (2004).

In Messenger's study of the Ocean Grove Holiness Camp, set up in the nineteenth century, he discusses 'muscular Christianity' and the idea that morality was a function of physicality as well as piety (1999, p. 67); his description of holiness 'at the beach' (1999, p. 71) and its popularity because of its beneficial physical effects points to a meantime theology in which spirituality is to be embodied rather than the body spiritualised: 'At Ocean Grove, God's hand was evident to the faithful both through the life-renewing waves and through the parted seas that led to new life on "the other shore" after death' (Messenger, 1999, p. 76). Hymns, popular in the 1880s Revival camp, all look forward to a time of homecoming, of anchoring in the harbour, to the day when the saved will see the 'perfect land where "shines one eternal day"' (Messenger, 1999, p. 77).

In the periods of Quaker history that followed the early enthusiasms of the 1650s, the Friends would need to devise their own meantime theology as evidence of the imminent Second Coming receded. The rest of this chapter focuses on the eighteenth and nineteenth centuries and how Quakers negotiated the failure of the prophecy about the transformation of the world.

Kathryn Damiano has argued that the sense of realising eschatology remained with the Friends into the eighteenth century but she claims this purely in terms of Quakers remaining a community living under Christ's guidance (1988, p. 96). According to Rosemary Moore (2001), Quakers were modifying their message as early as 1653/54. In 1656, James Nayler, one of the leaders of the early Quaker movement, re-enacted Christ's entry into Jerusalem by riding on a donkey into Bristol. He was tried for blasphemy, for believing he was Christ, and the accompanying scandal forced the Quakers to reassess their practice and self-presentation, particularly the ways in which God's leadings could and should be 'tested'. The confidence of the first years that Quakers were 'beyond falling' was being replaced by a sense of each being given a particular 'measure' of the Light of Christ that should not be overstepped or outrun.

The death of Oliver Cromwell in 1658 and the year of possibility that followed it gave a 'second wind' to Quaker eschatological zeal. Dorothy White, a prolific Quaker writer, wrote the following to Parliament in 1659:

> Friends, you that are of Parliament, hear the word of the Lord as it comes to me concerning you ... how your downfall is near, and this is now the word of the lord God of Hosts unto you all that are now sitting in Parliament, the Lord will overturn you by his Powerful Arm, for the decree of God and his purpose is ... to throw down and break up Parliaments ... God himself will rule, and bear rule in the hearts of men, and such as know God ... shall rule for God ... for God will throw down and overturn, root up and consume both root and branch of all your parliaments, until he hath brought in the Royal heir, the Prince of Peace, the Everlasting King of Righteousness and he will reign in the destruction of his enemies.
>
> (White, 1659)

However, the restoration of the monarchy in 1660 and the subsequent outlawing of Quaker worship through the 'Quaker Act' of 1662 forced the group to adopt a more pragmatic stance. Braithwaite claims 4,200 Quakers were jailed as a preventive measure following the Fifth Monarchist takeover of the City of London for a few days in 1661 (1919, p. 9). George Fox and twelve others then presented the King with a statement, similar to one Margaret Fell had written earlier, confirming the group's non-violence. This statement was to become symbolic of the testimony against war and, in the twentieth century, the peace testimony, but its public origins appear strategic.

When the potential signs of the plague and Great Fire of London in 1666, and the sinking of some of the Navy's best ships in the Thames by the Dutch navy in 1667 still failed to usher in the Kingdom, Quakers sensed that they too, along with the rest of Christianity, were going to have to face a further wait. The *Testimony to the Brethren* of 1666, a forceful instruction to local Meetings as to how to organise themselves and conduct their affairs and the template for the 'settling' of the Society, symbolises this move back from a sense of quickly unfolding endtime to a longer-term mission.

When, in 1676, Robert Barclay wrote his *Apology*, the first systematic and scholarly theology of the Quaker movement, his last chapter did not concern itself with eschatology as might be expected but with 'salutations and recreations' (2002). Indeed, as we shall see, Barclay says very little about eschatology and explicitly maintains a differently nuanced understanding of the Quaker place within the biblical understanding of time. Because of the importance of this work and its influence on future generations of Friends, we will consider what Barclay had to say in the areas of worship, baptism and communion.

Barclay considered worship the area Christians had most abused:

Hence it is that there is not anything relating to man's duty towards God which among all sorts of people hath been more vitiated, and in which the devil hath more prevailed, than in abusing man's mind concerning this thing: and as among many others, so among those called Christians, nothing hath been more out of order and more corrupted ...

(2002, p. 291)

In particular, Barclay denies there is 'any place in the true worship of God for that abominable superstition and idolatry the Popish mass' (ibid.) but he also considers that Protestant worship is not fully reformed and that their worship still comes from human will and spirit, rather than from the Spirit of God (ibid., p. 293). He begins by claiming that ceremonies which were valid under the age of the law are no longer valid under the age of the gospel. He critiques the setting-up of a particular preacher and the way in which worship is governed by the sermon, not by the promptings and breathings of the Spirit, and the way in which the sermon itself isn't thus prompted (ibid.).

Barclay claims all days are to be considered equal and that neither the Jewish Sabbath nor the first day of the week are to be set apart. This is also part of the old dispensation. Pragmatically, Quakers use the first day to worship and to rest, but also worship on other days (2002, p. 294).

True worship is about waiting upon God:

... the great work of one and all ought to be to wait upon God, and returning out of their own thoughts and imaginations, to feel the Lord's presence and know a 'gathering into his Name' indeed, where he is 'in the midst' according to his promise. And as everyone is thus gathered, and so met together inwardly in their spirits as well as outwardly in their persons, there the secret power and the virtue of life are known to refresh the soul, and the pure motions and breathings of God's Spirit are felt to arise ...

(Barclay, 2002, p. 296)

If words and prayers and praise do come (and worship consists neither in words nor in silence as such, but in a holy dependence of the mind upon God – ibid., p. 303), they will be from the Lord. If nothing is uttered, the worship is still true and will refresh and edify. Because silence is contrary to natural will, it only works when such will has been cast aside (thus acting as a certain reproof to will-worship – Col. 2:23). Barclay quotes Isaiah 30:20–21 to indicate the Teacher will be present when human will is absent:

... so there being also an inward quietness and retiredeness of mind, the witness of God ariseth in the heart, and the light of Christ shineth whereby the soul cometh to see its own condition. And there being many joined together in this same work, there is an inward travail and wrestling; and also, as a measure of Grace is abode in, an overcoming of the power and spirit of darkness; and thus we are often greatly strengthened and renewed in the spirits of our minds without a word, and we enjoy and possess the holy fellowship and 'communion of the body and blood of Christ,' by which our inward man is nourished and fed. Which makes us not to dote upon outward water and bread and wine in our spiritual things.

(2002, pp. 298–9)

Barclay justifies silent waiting and watching with scriptural references: Ps. 25:3, 27:14, 37:7, 9, 34, 69:6; Prov. 20:22; Isa. 30:18, 40:31, 42:23; Lam. 3:25–6; Hosea 12:6; Zeph. 3:8; Matt. 24:42, 25:13, 26:41; Mark 13:33, 35, 37; Luke 21:36; Acts 1:4–5, 20:31; 1 Cor. 16:13; Col. 4:2; 1 Thess. 5:5–6; 2 Tim. 4:5; 1 Pet. 4:7. However, his main justification for unprogrammed worship is that humanity has fallen from the faith and devised apostate liturgical forms. Quakers are following John 4:23–4, the true worshippers worshipping in spirit and in truth, part of a new covenant signalling the end to outward forms. To worship God in the Spirit is to worship God in the heart. The devil cannot counterfeit silent waiting upon God and humanity can leave its natural inclinations behind in this form. In that inward place, humanity is out of the devil's reach (2002, p. 311).

Barclay also suggests that at the time of Pentecost, the Apostles were silent until filled with the Holy Spirit when they began to talk in other tongues (Acts 2:1), and that Quaker worship has parallels with the worship of the early Church. The injunction to pray constantly (for example, 1 Thess. 5:17, Eph. 6:18, Luke 21:36) must, Barclay argues, practically speaking, be about inward prayer as constant outward prayer would be impossible. Outward prayer, rather, flows from inward prayer. Barclay ends his Proposition on worship with, amongst other verses, Isaiah 1:11–20 where God criticises old forms of worship and gives His people another opportunity:

> To what purpose is the multitude of your sacrifices unto me? Saith the Lord: I am full of the burnt offerings of rams, and the fat of fed beasts; and I delight not in the blood of bullocks, or of lambs, or of he goats. When ye come to appear before me, who hath required this at your hand, to tread my courts? Bring no more vain oblations; incense is an abomination unto me; the new moons and sabbaths, the calling of assemblies, I cannot away with; it is iniquity, even the solemn meeting. Your new moons and your appointed feasts my soul hateth: they are a trouble unto me; I am weary to bear them. And when ye spread forth your hands, I will hide mine eyes from you: yea, when ye make many prayers, I will not hear: your hands are full of blood. Wash you, make you clean; put away the evils of your doings from before mine eyes; cease to do evil; Learn to do well; seek judgment, relieve the oppressed, judge the fatherless, plead for the widow. Come now, and let us reason together, saith the Lord: though your sins be as scarlet, they shall be as white as snow; though they be red as crimson, they shall be as wool. If ye be willing and obedient, ye shall eat the good of the land. But if ye refuse and rebel, ye shall be devoured with the sword: for the mouth of the Lord hath spoken it.

Barclay justifies Quaker worship, then, with an argument based on scriptural reasoning relating to the formation of a new covenant with Christ, following the First Coming. He mentions nowhere the endtimes, but simply suggests that the liturgical forms of other Christians belong to an age now passed. In this, though, he is speaking from one meantime interpretation to another whilst claiming a restoration of apostolic Christianity (and thus, implicitly, the beginning of the possibility of the coming of the Kingdom with Pentecost).

On baptism, Barclay uses Matthew 15:6–9 as symbolic of his criticism of the apostate Church. Barclay claims other Christians hold on to borrowed practices so tenaciously: 'Which zeal, if they would but seriously examine it, they would find to be but the prejudice of education and the love of self more than of God or his pure worship' (2002, p. 345). Barclay also criticises the Catholic/Protestant debate over the number of sacraments, given the term 'sacrament' was originally pagan. If 'sacrament' is meant to refer to the 'outward visible sign of the conferral of inward grace', both Catholic and Protestant lists could be expanded, equally with the term 'ordinance' (2002, p. 346).

The one baptism of Ephesians 4:5 is the baptism of Christ, a baptism not by water but by the Spirit (1 Pet. 3:21). There are not two baptisms, one by water, one by Spirit, nor are there two parts to baptism (2002, p. 349). Barclay further quotes Romans 6:3–4, Galicians 3:27, and Colossians 2:12, to show that Paul is clear that baptism does not involve water. Christ never baptised with water, nor did he instruct others to do so, even in Matthew 28:19.

Barclay takes the passage from Hebrews 9:9–10 about maintaining outward ordinances until the time of reformation to refer to the age of the gospel which has come, to the new covenant established by the First Coming. As such, those who use outward baptism are practising the religion of the Jews.

Paul clearly claims he was not sent to baptise (1 Cor. 1:17) and he thanks God (1 Cor. 1:14) that he baptised so few. Barclay treats this selective baptism in the same way he treats Paul's circumcision of Timothy, that is, that Paul acted out of sympathy rather than commission. Opponents cannot take the passage from 1 Corinthians 1:17 to mean that baptism was also a possibility: 'Paul did not say "I was not sent principally to baptize", but, "I was not sent to baptize" ' (2002, p. 360).

Barclay concedes that the Apostles may have misunderstood Christ and wrongly initiated an outward ceremony but their use of it is not uniform. He argues with those who say that baptism means 'dipping in water' that the term is used figuratively and that baptism with Spirit and with fire, used by Christ, John and the Apostles would not then make sense. The real etymology is concerned with immersion but even those who call for water baptism do not all practise that. The badge of Christianity is their life, not an outward ceremony which was nowhere clearly instructed. Water baptism of infants is unwarranted (2002, p. 367).

Building on the idea of the two natures of humanity Barclay introduced in his proposition on worship, he claims that the communion of the body and blood of Christ is a mystery hidden from those still in their natural state. Given the apostate nature of humanity, this is why so many have followed a false outward rite, following the shadow rather than the substance (2002, p. 374). In John 6:32–71, Christ talks at length about participation in the body, flesh and blood of Christ as the way in which Christ communicates life and salvation to those who believe in him and receive him, and as the means to fellowship and communion with God (2002, p. 375). Nothing is said here about a ceremony. Rather, to Barclay, it is clear that the body, flesh and blood referred to by Christ are spiritual. In 1 Corinthians 16:17, those united with the Lord become one Spirit, not one flesh, argues Barclay. The passage in 1 Corinthians 10:3–4 makes it clear that there is a spiritual body of Christ as there was a physical body too.

To come to Christ and be fed is not about an outward ceremony but a true turning to the Light so that the seed of righteousness is raised up and rebirth occurs which will naturally feed upon and be nourished by the spiritual body of Christ, as in Revelation 3:20 (2002, p. 380). This is the true communion, available individually but felt particularly when assembled together to wait upon the Lord. (Note that Barclay is not here talking about the supper of the marriage of the Lamb.)

Barclay then proceeds to critique the confusion of other Christians in trying to connect the supper of the Lord with the ceremony Christ used before his death, visible in the other churches in three versions: Roman Catholic transubstantiation (where the bread and wine are transformed by God into the real body and blood of Christ), Lutheran consubstantiation (where the bread and wine coexist with the body and blood of Christ), and Calvinistic virtualism (in which the bread and wine spiritualises the body and blood). Barclay claims all three ideas suffer from trying to connect communion to the outward body of Christ. Their second error is that they link communion with the sharing of bread and wine by Christ before his death. Matthew and Mark mention this meal but not an instruction from Christ to continue the practice. However, even the act of remembrance is not the same as true communion, Barclay argues (2002, p. 386). Additionally, remembrance does not require communion.

When, in 1 Corinthians 10:16, the word 'communion' is linked with bread, it does not refer to outward bread, such as in John 6:35. In 1 Corinthians 11:23–9, the instruction by Paul to eat the bread and drink the cup in remembrance (not communion as in Revelation 3:20) is not an instruction to institute an obligatory ceremony. Rather, it is a call to enact this remembrance in a prepared manner and not to abuse the ceremony as Paul felt the Church at Corinth had. Thus, even as an act of remembrance, as opposed to true communion, there is no scriptural support to suggest that this is a ceremony Christ wished the Church to sustain. There is neither scriptural authority to argue otherwise or the authority of Apostolic succession to heed, given the fall of the Church into apostasy.

Paul's 'whenever you drink it' (1 Cor. 11:25) is not an instruction to drink but a reminder to remembrance should you happen to drink. The instruction in Luke to 'do this in remembrance of me' was a way of helping the disciples through Christ's suffering and death. It was equivalent to the ceremony of foot-washing which is not carried out daily or weekly in churches because there is no explicit instruction in Scripture to do so. Similarly, the Church has not instituted the abstention from meat and blood referred to in Acts 15:29 or the anointing of the sick with oil (James

5:14). Equally, those who do perform the outward ceremony of the breaking of bread and sharing of wine do not carry it out as Christ did, in the evening (2002, p. 394). As is usual, Barclay attacks the position of other Christians for their mistaken exegesis and for their inconsistencies.

Interestingly, given what we have argued above in Chapters 1 and 2, Barclay suggests that the phrase 'till he come' in 1 Corinthians 11:26 need not refer to the Second Coming but refers to Christ's inward visitation (2002, p. 401). In this, Barclay makes it clear that he does not believe that the Second Coming is unfolding in the way in which Fox did. Neither, then, does he argue that the ceremony of remembrance is redundant. Rather, he posits true communion as unrelated to what Paul is talking about in this passage and additionally concludes that a ceremony of remembrance is not instructed by Scripture beyond a means to help the weak. External rites are not part of the new covenantal dispensation (Col. 2:20–23, Heb. 9:10), the new inward covenant expressed in Isaiah 59:21, and in Jeremiah 31:31–4, repeated in Hebrews 10:11 (Barclay, 2002, p. 404). Thus, the passages we have used above to outline the first Friends' belief in a new covenant with a focus on the endtimes are used by Barclay to also refer to a new covenant initiated by the First Coming, but one with less emphasis on the endtimes. Gurney used the same device 150 years later (1979; see Chapter 4 below) and John Punshon 320 years later (2001). Barclay uses standardised Quaker scriptural preferences (Jer. 31:31–4, Rev. 3:20) but modifies the message away from one associated with the endtimes, a

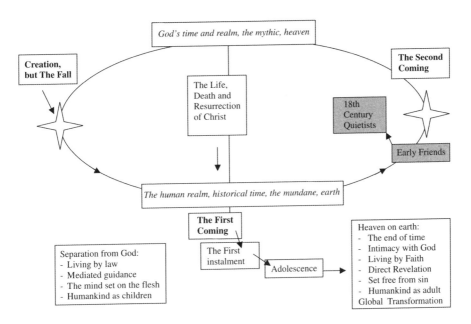

Figure 3.1 Eighteenth-century Friends and the biblical understanding of time

manoeuvre that is then used consistently by succeeding generations of Quakers. He also treats 1 Corinthians 11:23–9 differently. In this, Barclay alters the Quaker understanding of time or reflects the changed Quaker understanding (although George Fox's message remains unchanged until his death in 1691).

Barclay's work was not about how to expect the end of the world but rather how to live faithfully in this one. He also modified the doctrine of perfection to allow always for room for further growth: 'This is not a perfection that has no room for further growth ... It is a perfection which is proportionable and answerable to man's measure' (Barclay, 2002, p. 207). Barclay also enshrined the idea that every individual had a singular day of visitation, after which there was no possibility of salvation (ibid., p. 119). How long 'a day' is would vary from individual to individual but it could not be summoned up by the individual (ibid., pp. 127–8) and it was a sole opportunity for salvation.

Gwyn has described a puritan spirituality of anxiety (1995, p. 81) rooted in the uncertainty of predestination but here we can see the beginnings of a Quaker one. After the death of Barclay in the early 1690s, William Penn had his complete works published and they became a standard text. The children of the first Quakers, now living in Quaker households could see that their forebears had had an experience they needed to emulate: 'I saw closely in that Day ... that unless I became acquainted with the Power that had Wrought a Change and Alteration in my dear parents ... I should be miserable and undone forever' (O'Shea, 1993, p. 45).

Influenced by French Quietism, the idea of becoming merely a vessel for God became predominant within what has been called Quietist Quakerism, the period of Quaker theology between the 1690s and the 1830s. The human emotions were not to be trusted, existing only on the natural plane rather than the supernatural plane aspired to. From the quaking so central to Tarter's analysis (2001), Quakers became wary of the physical and the emotional. From being co-agents with God over and against the world, to negotiating with the world in the Restoration period, the Quietist Quakers became nervous of both God and the world (see Tousley's excellent study on convincement narratives for an analysis of the changes between first- and second-generation Friends, 2003).

The world was a corrupt and corrupting place and could distract the believer from being open to their day of visitation, or from true obedience, a point made by Sarah Lynes Grubb in the following extract from 1780: 'I am often afraid lest by indulging my own ideals of what is good, and not labouring after a total resignation of mind ... I should frustrate the divine intention, which may be to humble and reduce self more than flesh and blood would point out' (Jones, 1921, p. 68). Nothingness of self was a standard aspiration, as this loving letter from Richard Shackleton to his daughter in 1773 reveals:

> Mayst thou, dear child, be preserved in simplicity and nothingness of self, in humility and lowliness of mind, seeking diligently after, and waiting steadily for, the inward experience of that which is unmixedly good. This is the way to be helped along, from

day to day, through one difficulty and proving after another, to the end of our wearisome pilgrimage.

(Jones, 1921, p. 65)

Thus the eighteenth-century Quaker was one continually wary of disobedience. Damiano tells stories of people, felt drawn by God into marriage, nevertheless waiting for a further prompting before acting on the leading. In one case Damiano mentions, six years passed between the first prompting and marriage (1988, p. 184).

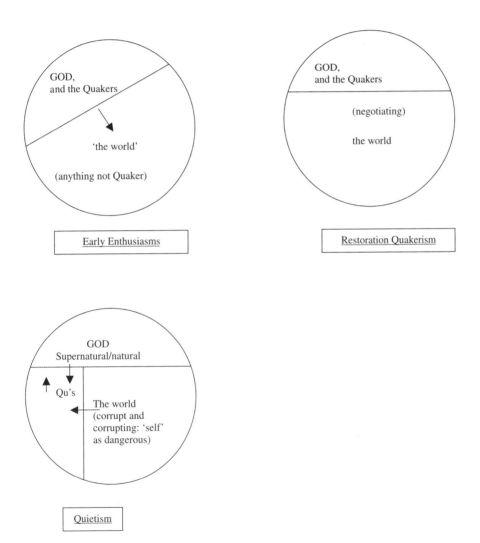

Figure 3.2 Early, Restoration, and Quietistic Quaker understandings of 'the world'

In the case of Catherine Phillips, it took her 23 years before she was sure of the choice of her marriage partner (1988, p. 183).

In terms of worship, such anxiety over faithfulness could lead to a lack of ministry, although not to minister in the face of a prompting would also be falling short. In general though, it seems that worship grew shorter and quieter. In some Meetings, monitors were appointed to wake the sleeping. The dramatic experiences of the first Friends were not felt in the same vivid and transforming ways in the subsequent centuries.

As early as 1662, Quaker practice was being challenged. John Perrot, one of John Luffe's companions in the mission to Rome, suggested that the times of Meeting and the removal (or not) of hats should only be guided by God. This challenge was short-lived and the dangers of individual revelation compromising the unity of the movement, visible too in the Nayler incident, resulted in a clear rule of corporate testing of individual revelation.

From the 1670s, Ministers required certificates of release and there was advice against judging 'the church', that is, the Quakers. Thus a group who had begun by obedience to Divine instruction to preach against worldly and outward forms had set up its own. Ministry and Ministers, while guided by God, were regulated by the movement (Bauman, 1983, pp. 142–7). At the same time, criticism of ministry was still to be left until the end of Meeting thus at least giving a 'Divine potential' to ministry, and Ministers were given a raised bench to sit on when the first Meeting Houses were built in the 1670s, a symbol of the co-option of their authority into the new management of Quakerism. Architecture did not reflect the ideal of the free ministry. In Weberian terms, as Bauman points out, this was all a classic example of the routinisation of charisma/prophecy.

Ministry may have become less frequent. There is the oft-quoted example of 22 consecutive Meetings in Dublin without a word spoken (Jones, 1921, p. 63). At the same time, John Smith of Philadelphia heard 657 prayers or sermons, an average of four per meeting between January 1745 and January 1746 (Frost, 1973, p. 38). What is clear is that ministry developed a distinct intonation, symbolic of the difference between speaker, God, and vessel, the Minister. One visitor to Meeting in 1750 reported the following which occured after an hour and a quarter of silence:

> Finally, one of the two ... old men in the front pew rose, removed his hat, turned hither and yon, and began to speak, but so softly that even in the middle of the church, which was not large, it was impossible to hear anything except the confused murmur of the words. Later he began to talk a little louder, but so slowly that four or five minutes elapsed between the sentences; finally the words came both louder and faster. In their preaching, the Quakers have a peculiar mode of expression, which is half singing with a strange cadence and accent, and ending each cadence, as it were, with a half or ... a full sob. Each cadence consists of two, three, or four syllables, but sometimes more, according to the demand of the words and means; e.g. my friends/ put in your mind/ we/ do nothing/ good of our selves/ without God's/ help and assistance/ etc. In the beginning the sobbing is not heard so plainly, but the deeper the

speaker gets into his sermon the stronger becomes the sobbing between the cadences. The speaker today made no gestures, but turned in various directions; occasionally he placed one hand on his cheek; and during most of the sermon kept buttoning and unbuttoning his vest with right hand … When he stood for a while using his sing-song method he changed his manner of delivery and spoke in a more natural way, or as our ministers do when they say a prayer. Shortly afterwards, however, he began again his half-singing mode of expression, and at the end, just as he was speaking at his best, he stopped abruptly, sat down, and put on his hat.

(Green, 1978, p. 42)

In looking at the Orthodox tradition, David Martin outlines the ways that a secular aesthetic and all the 'artifical tensions and releases created by consonance and dissonance' can be created by using a particular style of inflection and prolongation (2002, p. 48). The same subordination to the sacred is evident in this extract.

Given that their situation was now clearly one of the meantime, it is interesting that these Friends did not decide to alter a liturgical form so rooted in an experience of the unfolding Second Coming. Friends could have quite legitimately begun to break the bread 'till he come' given their movement back from the endtime moment. What they did however was follow Barclay in emphasising the intimacy of their relationship with God and its direct nature without connecting it explicitly to the Second Coming.

Damiano states that the Quietist experience of the 'daily nourishment of the inward person by Christ within whom he dwells' as inherently related to a realised eschatology (1988, p. 156). The connection would be an obvious one, drawing as early Friends did on Revelation 3:20, but Barclay doesn't make it and neither do the Quietist Friends.

Barclay and the Quakers who followed him de-coupled a sense of endtime and a sense of intimacy. What then was to help this part of the people of God remain faithful? It is true that those with 'the gift of ministry' were 'recorded' as such after 1722 and travelling Ministers moved about with a certificate of release, but these Friends did not lead worship. Instead of adopting the methods used by the rest of Christianity such as a set-apart people (priests), sacred buildings (churches), times and seasons (the Christian calendar), and outward sacraments, they maintained a collective separation. Earlier Quaker insights such as the 'plain' speech ('thee' and 'thou' to everyone, eschewing the more polite 'you', being literal and economic in speech, not using titles, and using numbers for the days and months) and plain dress became highly formalised. In 1714, even hair was taken under the care of the Meeting: 'If any Friend wants hair, they should acquaint the men's meeting they belong to, and have approbation and consent, before they get any' (Vann, 1969, p. 192).

Such a marked separation from the world, paradoxically expressed through outward forms, maintained a sense of Quakers as God's vanguard and chosen people as opposed to people of 'the world'. It also lent itself to notions of being in one group or the other and the practice of 'disownment', a practice that became increasingly used as the list of potential offences grew throughout the eighteenth century (Marietta, 1984). In particular, Quakers were disowned for marrying before a priest, either to a non-Quaker or a Quaker without their parents' and therefore the Meeting's permission. As more and more energy went into the maintenance and presentation of purity, less went into mission and numbers declined. However, this only affirmed the narrow path of the truly faithful. It was these behavioural codes that underpinned a meantime practice rather than any explicit liturgical reform.

Friends often quoted Titus in defence of their peculiarities:

> For the grace of God that bringeth salvation hath appeared to all men, teaching us that, denying ungodliness and worldly lusts, we should live soberly, righteously, and godly, in this present world. Looking for that blessed hope, and the glorious appearing of the great God and our Saviour Jesus Christ; Who gave himself for us, that he might redeem himself from all iniquity, and purify unto himself a peculiar people, zealous of good works.
>
> (Tit. 2:11–14)

This is a passage that looks towards a future endtime, not of finding the risen Christ within. In this way, the basis for the unprogrammed liturgy had changed (Quakers were still in the world but not of it, but they also saw no immediate chance of moving into the next), and this would lay the liturgy itself open to change by future generations of Friends. The next chapter charts these further shifts.

CHAPTER 4

Different Confessions, Different Liturgies

The Evangelical period that was to replace Quietist Quakerism in Britain in the nineteenth century and form its own tradition in the United States brought with it new understandings of how best to help the Quaker people of God remain faithful. The Modernist tendencies within this Evangelical Quakerism would further divide Evangelical Quakerism in the US and create a Liberal Quakerism to replace Evangelical domination in Britain. This chapter charts these shifts and how they were played out in changing understandings of Quaker liturgy.

The driving forces behind the gradual increase of evangelical influence within the Quaker movement were manifold. For those Quakers who had become part of the new urban elite through success in trade, the Quaker 'peculiarities' of plain dress and plain speech felt increasingly burdensome. The effectiveness of these behavioural codes at maintaining a sense of separation from 'the world' felt anachronistic to those who felt more and more at home with Christians of other denominations and their spirit of revival. In other words, their sense of 'the world' had changed from being 'anything not Quaker' to 'anything not Christian' and they no longer saw the need to be so 'hedged in' around other Christians. For these Friends, Quakerism was no longer the true church but part of the true (Christian) church. Some converted out of Quakerism, others strove to reform the movement and bring it up to date.

As Evangelical theology became more accepted, with it came the need to spread the good news. In this regard, the peculiarities were seen as an obstacle to mission. Who would want to join a group that required you to dress and speak differently? A battle began between the old guard of Quietism and the new Evangelical thinking over 'the hedge' and its value. The stakes were perceived to be high on both sides. For the Quietists, lowering the hedge would lead to corruption and apostasy. Already, in the words of Moses West, in his 1780 *Treatise on Marriage*, the violators of endogamy who brought their non-Quaker spouses to Meeting provided 'an inlet to much degeneracy, and mournfully affected the minds of all those who labour under a living Concern for the Good of all, and the prosperity of Truth upon Earth' (Marietta, 1984, p. 65). For Quakers themselves to lose accountability and constraint on these issues would lead only to disaster. As one Quaker put it, 'I would rather die as a dog in a ditch than say "*You*" to a single person' (Isichei, 1967, p. 171).

For the Evangelical wing in Britain, retaining the hedge would lead to extinction. By 1859, a group that had once perhaps numbered sixty, was 13,859 strong (Isichei,

1970, p. 112). In terms of the advice on plain dress and speech, *The Friend* reported of the 1860 Yearly Meeting:

> All appeared to agree that it was the Christian duty of the Society to maintain a testimony to simplicity of dress and language. The only difference of view was in regard to the most effective way of doing so: whether by enacting and maintaining special rules of conduct in this respect; or by enforcing the general principle, and leaving the details to the convictions of the individual conscience.
>
> (*The Friend*, 1860, **18**, p. 104)

Finally, in 1861, the latter part of the fourth query on plainness of speech, behaviour and apparel was abolished, Friends claiming they could live this testimony inwardly: 'a tailor's scissors could never make a Quaker', one Friend claimed (*The British Friend*, 1859, **17**, p. 151). Plainness had been turned into 'simplicity' and the individual conscience had replaced corporate clarity.

In 1860, endogamy was abolished, and by 1880, a third of all Quaker marriages were to non-Quakers ('Yearly Meeting Minutes', 1880). Without disownment for this offence, and with the increased mission work Evangelical thinking brought with it, numbers rose after 1865. These two reforms, on plainness and endogamy, allowed for the first time the possibility of a Quaker private life outside of the Meeting House.

What is interesting is that in Britain the peculiarity of worship remained untouched. Water baptism was briefly discussed at Yearly Meeting in 1837 and 1838 (Isichei, 1970, pp. 49–50), but the leading proponents of Evangelical theology within British Quakerism made no bid to change the liturgical form. Indeed Joseph John Gurney, perhaps the most prominent of the first wave of British Evangelical Quakers, remained a Quaker rather than convert to Anglicanism because of his belief in the efficacy of unprogrammed worship.

Gurney, in his *Observations on the Distinguishing Views and Practices of the Society of Friends* (1979 [1834]), approached Quaker theology in as systematic a way as Barclay had and using similar arguments. In the seventh edition, used as the basis for the version quoted here, twelve chapters outlined Quaker faith and practice. We shall focus on his treatment of the outward sacraments and silent worship, his argument that 'God *may* be acceptably and profitably worshipped without the intervention of a single typical ceremony, and without the necessary or constant aid of any human ministry' (Gurney 1979, p. 73).

First, Gurney gives the Friends their authority for their peculiarities, citing in particular the key Quaker text, Jeremiah 31:31–4 (Gurney, 1979, p. 82). This manner of unmediated guidance has led the Quakers to their peculiarity comprising of the

> ... disuse of all typical observances in the worship of God: their refusal to recognize any ministry in connexion with divine worship, which they do not conceive to be dictated by the immediate influence of the Holy Spirit: their acceptance of the public

ministry of females; their objection to the human ordination, and also to the paying or hiring of preachers: their custom of silent worship: their abstaining from all warfare, both offensive and defensive, and from the use of oaths: their plainness in speech, behaviour, and apparel.

(Gurney 1979, p. 96)

All has come through obedience to the inward guide in a new covenantal relationship with God made possible through Christ. It is in his Chapter 4 that Gurney focuses 'on the disuse of all typical rites in the worship of God', that is, 'baptism with water' and 'the sacrament of the Lord's supper' and how 'they are not in accordance with the entire spirituality of the gospel dispensation' (Gurney 1979, pp. 99–100).

Gurney's first point is that Scripture suggests that a new dispensation has been made available, and that old forms of rite are to be replaced. He quotes John 4:21–4 including 'the hour cometh, and now is, when the true worshippers shall worship the Father *in spirit and in truth*' (Gurney 1979, p. 101, original emphasis). The new worship was not to consist in 'outward rites of a formal and ceremonial nature' (ibid., p. 102). Gurney cites Hebrews 10:5–9: 'he taketh away the first, that he may establish the second' (ibid., p. 104) and from Colossians 2:20 Paul questioning their subjection to ordinances, and argues that baptism was a Jewish ceremony, a cleansing upon conversion (ibid., p. 107), the new baptism *of* conversion which Christ introduced.

Gurney then turns his attention to the claim in John 3:3–5 that 'except a man be born of water and of the spirit, he cannot enter into the kingdom of God.' He argues that the second part of the sentence is an explanatory repetition of the first, and does not refer to a second separate process (ibid., p. 121). When in Titus 3:3–6 we read of 'washing of regeneration, and renewing of the Holy Ghost', Gurney argues that these are part of a single spiritual process, similarly with the passage in Hebrews 10:19–22 (ibid., p. 123).

Gurney lists the typical selection of Matthew 3:11, 12, Luke 3:16–17, Mark 1:7–8, Acts 1:5 and 1 Corinthians 12:12, 13 to argue that the new baptism is a baptism by the Spirit. Finally, Gurney claims that even where the Apostles use water baptism, they don't do so uniformly, for example, as with Paul and the Church at Corinth (ibid., p. 142). He also contends that the Lord's Supper is borrowed from the Jewish rite of Passover. He uses 1 Corinthians 11:20 to claim that it is neither a ceremony involving the real body and blood (that is, transubstantiation) or the spiritualised body and blood (for example, the Anglican position), that is, that it is not 'heavenly food'. Rather, Gurney suggests, it is representative, and commemorative (ibid., pp. 147–8).

Gurney uses the instructive passage from 1 Corinthians 11: 23–6 and adds the next three verses, up to 29 as an instruction, not to institute a ceremony but to avoid the abuse of it, as the Corinthians had been doing. He claims that Luke 22:19, 20 is not about ordaining a central part of worship, and that Matthew and Mark omitted the words, 'do this in remembrance of me' as they were not important (ibid., p. 155).

Equally, he suggests that the correct emphasis of the phrase 'Do this in remembrance of me' should be on the word 'me'. That is, Jesus is trying to ensure the remembrance of him as opposed to remembrance of anything else, again referring to the borrowed nature of the practice (ibid., p. 156).

Finally, Gurney turns his attention to the 'Till he come' of the 1 Corinthians 11:26 passage. He does not claim that the Second Coming is unfolding, but does claim, from Revelation 3:20 that the true supper is available, and that it is an inward one (ibid., p. 165). In other words, Gurney is using Jeremiah 31:31–4 and Revelation 3:20 to uphold a sense of an inward intimacy with Christ, as early Friends did, but one held in the meantime, not the soon-coming endtime. Thus, Gurney suggests that the earnest of Christ's First Coming has introduced a new kind of covenantal relationship with God as foretold in Jeremiah. For Gurney, as with Barclay, the emphasis is not pointing towards the Second Coming. In this, Quaker Christianity is in the same place as the rest of Christianity in its sense of where it is operating within God's time, that is, a place of waiting. Where Gurney differs is in his reading of the Gospels regarding the necessity or even suggestion of outward rites. Whilst he believes Friends are correct in their interpretation of Scripture, he ends the chapter in an ecumenical spirit, asking Friends not to judge those who continue these practices as God accepts the sincere heart and 'is pleased to bless a variety of means to a variety of conditions' (ibid., p. 168). Gurney's position needs to be less dogmatic than that of the early Friends because he is agreeing with other Christians on where they are in time, and only disagreeing on how they have been instructed to wait. Early Friends felt the time of waiting was over and that the other churches were holding people back from experiencing the unfolding endtime and preparing for the Day of Judgement.

In his chapter on worship, Gurney cites three aspects of worship as central: entire humiliation and complete prostration before the divine Majesty; waiting, and being taught. He gives scriptural examples for all three in terms of how silence is the most adequate mean to these ends. For humiliation, he uses the examples of those chastised into silence, from Psalm 39:2, 9 and Jeremiah 8:14, also using Habakkuk 2:20 and Zecheriah 2:13. As examples of waiting, he uses Psalm 27:14, Psalm 37:7, implying from the Hebrew, that waiting is meant to be silent, and Revelation 8:1 (the silence of expectation) (ibid., p. 299). Finally, in terms of being taught, he simply quotes the phrase from Psalm 46:10 'Be Still and Know that I am God'. He ends by arguing that Scripture does not specify any particular form of worship.

The division between Evangelical and Quietist Friends was not simply about the outward markers of faith, or numbers, or even between denominational and sectarian understandings of church. The basic tension was over the authority of Scripture against the authority of the Inward Light. Early Friends had found Scripture validated and confirmed their revelation but Quietist Friends felt too close a study of Scripture a worldly and carnal pursuit. The more Evangelical Friends were wary of the notion of the Inward Light, could not find it validated by Scripture and felt it could be reduced to mere 'impressions of our own imagination'

(Mingins, 2003, p. 58). In this way, they criticised the Quietists for the very snare the Quietists were trying to avoid, that is, self-led spirituality.

In 1835, Isaac Crewdson, a prominent Manchester Friend, published *A Beacon to the Society of Friends* in which he declared that the Inward Light was a delusional notion. His ultra-Evangelical position and harsh criticism of a concept still dear to many Friends led to conflict in Manchester and in Kendal and his eventual resignation, along with about four hundred Friends (the biggest schism in the history of British Quakerism). Freed from the constraint of Quakerism, the Crewdsonites, or Beaconites as they were known, built a large chapel in Manchester and developed their own ecclesiology with deacons and elders and introduced programmed worship with hymns and a sermon (Isichei, 1970, p. 49).

This was the last challenge to the unprogrammed form in Britain. A smaller Conservative schism in 1869 in response to the abolition of the peculiarities had no need to protest over liturgical reform, for other than a shortening again of worship time to an hour and a half, there hadn't been any.

In the US, the nineteenth century produced far greater diversity and the beginnings of what would become by the mid-twentieth century six types of Quakerism, divided between programmed and unprogrammed.

In 1827, the Philadelphia Yearly Meeting divided in two and both a 'Hicksite' (named after Elias Hicks) and an 'Orthodox' Yearly Meeting claimed to be the true inheritors of the tradition. The division, which spread to other Yearly Meetings, was sociological (Doherty, 1967) as well as theological (Hamm, 1988, pp. 15–20) but can be simplified in terms of the Hicksites representing a behavioural definition of Quakerism, the Orthodox representing an (Evangelical) doctrinal definition. Whilst the Hicksite branch would thus face further small divisions over form, the Orthodox would face further divisions over doctrine and right belief. When the British Friend Joseph John Gurney came to the United States for three years in 1837, he drew the criticism of John Wilbur, an Orthodox New England Friend, for understating the importance of the Inward Light alongside Scripture. In 1843, Wilbur and his supporters found themselves disowned from New England Yearly Meeting and they set up their own. As with the earlier schism, this conflict over interpretation and definition of Quakerism spread to other Yearly Meetings. By 1854, for example, there were three Yearly Meetings in Ohio – Hicksite, Gurneyite and Wilburite.

All three branches retained unprogrammed worship. However, some Evangelical Friends sought change. Particularly concerned by the dangers of Hicksism (a fear which had also fuelled the Crewdsonites in Britain), Friends in Indiana had started First Day Schools before 1840, and home prayer meetings in the 1850s, encouraged by accounts of interdenominational revival meetings in the *Friends Review* (Wood, 1978, p. 56). In 1860, at Indiana Yearly Meeting, a special Sunday evening Meeting was held specifically without the leadership and preaching of the recorded ministers: 'At least 1,500 persons attended the special service, no fewer than 120 testified or prayed, and one individual sang a hymn, a practice unheard of in Quaker

Meetings for the preceding 150 years' (Wood, 1978, p. 57). The Civil War delayed further and fuller revivalism until about 1867 (ibid.). Criticism grew of traditional practices, such as kneeling to pray, with the rest of the Meeting removing their hats and the distinct nasal sing-song tone of ministry. Revival Meetings grew in popularity, high in emotion and in numbers. In the 1870s, General Meetings were set up by a number of Yearly Meetings to try and offer a teaching ministry to the newcomers and to offer a less formal devotional Meeting. Within a year or so, the second aspect had taken over from the first and revival Meetings at which participants were encouraged to follow the Spirit, even if it led to 'the ways of other denominations' (Wood, 1978, p. 63). Singing (only as led by the Spirit and rarely accompanied before about 1890), preaching, prayer, testimony and the use of the altar call and mourners' benches became commonplace and eventually became part of Monthly Meeting activities.

This devotional work by Evangelical Friends led to new challenges. Meetings grew, often considerably (Hamm, 1988, p. 125), and preaching increased, but Meetings lacked the means to educate and nurture the newcomers. There was a danger of the enthusiasm being greater than the means to sustain it. This branch of Quakerism doubled in size, from 45,000 to 90,000 Friends between 1850 and 1900 (Wood, 1978, p. 71). Wood lists four options facing the Yearly Meetings experiencing such revival. They could a) cut back on these activities, b) separate the membership of the more formal silent worship from the other Meetings, as happened in England with its evening Home Mission Meetings, c) set up pastoral committees, or d) where Meetings could and where they agreed, allow them to release a pastor for service (Wood, 1978, p. 67). The Meetings typically preferred the third option but most were to finally adopt the fourth as the need for pastoral care outstripped provision. This wasn't without controversy and the rival Quaker journals *Friends Review* and *Christian Worker* traded editorials. However by the 1890, most of the Midwest Gurneyite Yearly Meetings had accepted this practice (Wood, 1978, p. 69).

In short, Pastoral Committees were set up to help with the teaching ministry and were soon replaced by single-person pastorates:

> Every church must be provided with a living gospel ministry, someone whose business it is to care for the flock; to visit the sick – to look after the newly awakened, and lead them to the feet of the Savior; to encourage the new converts, pray with, and for them, and to teach them the way of salvation more perfectly; to visit the membership of the church at their homes, socially and religiously; share with them their joys and sorrows; enter into sympathy with them in their trials and difficulties; see that none stray from the fold and become prodigals; reprove those who sin, and win them back if possible to the path of duty; if differences arise between brethren, see that the gospel order is followed speedily, that the matter be adjusted and settled in privacy before it be known abroad and the cause suffer loss.
>
> (Siler, 1887, p. 401)

The Church needed explicit leadership. By 1900 all but one Gurneyite Yearly Meeting had Pastoral Meetings (Hamm, 1988, p. 127). The adoption of Pastors soon led to the adoption of programming. Pastors were not priests. What had begun as a reaction to the formalism of unprogrammed worship led to a Spirit-led pre-programming. The sense of spiritual intimacy was maintained. The ministry in its fullest sense still belonged to all, but Pastors were those men or women, who had been bestowed particular gifts. Ministers were released for service, most paid for their ministry: ' ... on the one hand, the Gospel should never be preached for money (Acts 20:33–35), on the other, it is the duty of the church to make such provision that it shall never be hindered for want of it' ('Declaration of Faith Issued by the Richmond Conference', 1887).

Key to the Evangelical theology on both sides of the Atlantic was the central role it gave Scripture:

> It has ever been, and still is, the belief of the Society of Friends that the Holy Scriptures of the Old and New Testament were given by inspiration of God; that, therefore, there can be no appeal from them to any other authority whatsoever ... The Scriptures are the only divinely authorized record of doctrines which we are bound as Christians to accept ...
>
> ('Declaration of Faith ...', 1887)

In turn, this led to a more explicit and self-aware stance on the Second Coming. Hamm divides Gurneyite Friends into two sorts: Revival/Holiness and Reform/Modernist (1988). The former group were those influenced by the inter-denominational camp revivals with their emphasis on holiness as the goal of the Christian life. These Friends were more guarded from the world and less open to working with non-Christians or 'the world's people' on social justice issues. For example, they saw no point in maintaining plain dress when deists and heathen (that is, Hicksites) were dressed similarly (Hamm, 1988, p. 85). Equally, they wouldn't join in with the likes of Hicksites in joint projects. Hamm reports these Friends claiming football as unworthy of the attention of the sanctified and that union cards were the mark of the beast (1988, p. 164). In general, these Friends looked to Christ's Second Coming ahead of the thousand-year rule of the Saints prophesied in Revelation 20:1–4. That is, they were pre-millennialist.

The Reform/Modernist Friends were more open to the world (see Figure 4.1), wished to bring Quakerism into the world more, and saw the mission of the Church to usher in the thousand-year rule of the saints prior to the Second Coming. In this way, they were post-millennialist as Christ would come after the rule of the saints. Both pre- and post-millennial tendencies were, however, explicitly meantime positions. They explicitly looked ahead to the coming of the kingdom and made no claims as to the immediacy of the Second Coming. In this sense, these Friends adopted a standard Christian position of optimistic waiting.

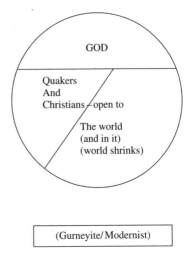

(Gurneyite/Modernist)

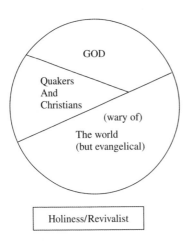

Holiness/Revivalist

Figure 4.1 Evangelical Quaker understandings of 'the world'

The Richmond 'Declaration of Faith', adopted by Gurneyite Yearly Meetings encompassing both holiness and modernist tendencies included the following on the Second Coming:

> We believe, according to the Scriptures, that there shall be a resurrection from the dead, both of the just and unjust (Acts 24:15), and that God hath appointed a day in which He will judge the world in righteousness, by Jesus Christ whom He hath ordained (Acts 17:31) ... We sincerely believe, not only a resurrection in Christ from

the fallen and sinful state here, but a rising and ascending into glory with Him thereafter, that when He at last appears we may appear with him in glory.

('Declaration of Faith Issued by the Richmond Conference', 1887)

The tense is future. The section of the 'Declaration' entitled 'The First Day of the Week' gives thanks for God's setting-apart of one day of the week for 'the purpose of holy rest, religious duties, and public worship' (ibid.). It is a different reading of time from the continuous end of time for early Friends. In the diagram used earlier to denote a biblical timeline, these Evangelical Friends have moved to an explicit meantime position, attempting to remain faithful between First and Second Comings.

Thus, the liturgical reform they undertook in adopting programmed worship was as appropriate and as logical as the Quietist behavioural codes they abolished. If the Church is to help the people of God remember what they are about in the meantime, any effective means is legitimate. Indeed, following Scripture as they did, they could have instituted further reform. In particular, the continued proscription of outward communion is interesting. What prevented this was the continued sense of inward and spiritual intimacy with God.

The 'Declaration' claimed the following:

> We would express our continued conviction that our Lord appointed no outward rite or ceremony for observance in His church ... The eating of His body and the drinking of

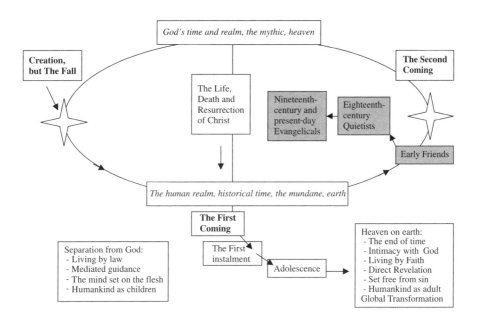

Figure 4.2 Evangelical Quakers and the biblical understanding of time

His blood cannot be an outward act. They truly partake of them who habitually rest
upon the sufferings and death of our Lord as their only hope, and to whom the
indwelling Spirit gives to drink of the fullness that is Christ. It is this inward and
spiritual partaking that is the true supper of the Lord.

('Declaration of Faith ...', 1887)

In other words, these Friends questioned, after Barclay and Gurney, the instruction to
this ordinance and questioned the meaning of John 6 when it was taken by other
churches in an outward way. Later in this section, they quote Revelation 3:20,
'Behold, I stand at the door and knock, if any man hear my voice, and open the door, I
will come in to him, and sup with him, and he with me', in order to justify an
unmediated communion, 'unfettered by any outward rite or ceremonial, to partake
together of the body that was broken and the blood that was shed for them, without the
gates of Jerusalem' ('Declaration of faith', 1887). They do not quote 1 Corinthians
11:26 and instead spiritualise communion. Equally they do not suggest, logically
given their explicit sense of waiting, that 'the command' to share the body and the
blood is anachronistic because they don't believe the command comes from Christ or
that Paul meant to establish a necessary outward ceremony anyway. In this sense, their
use of Revelation 3:20 is different from the way the first Friends used it. It is not used
to point towards the marriage supper of the Lamb but rather to an inward communion
and away from the other churches' interpretation of the manner of remembrance the
other Christians saw as instructed by Christ and by Paul. In this, they follow Barclay.

Whilst Gurney was wedded to unprogrammed worship, some Holiness Friends
declared silent worship was a sin when praise would be more appropriate (Hamm,
1988, p. 85). This represented a tension between Wesleyan Holiness teaching and
its emphasis on the expression of testimony and the inward communion of historic
Quakerism. Taking Gurney's notion of intimacy rather than his views on worship
and mistrustful of the ideas of the 'Inward Light', silent waiting could appear a
curious way to worship. In its formalised form, it had perhaps lost the power of the
intimacy with God that Revivalist Friends found through other means. In other
ways, they retained traditional Quaker theological insights. Pastors were not priests
and they suggested that George Fox and the early Quakers were proto-pastors
(Siler, 1887). There were still no outward sacraments, even if the reasoning against
an outward Lord's Supper was different, and the emphasis on holiness or
sanctification was easily compared with the perfectionist theology of early Friends.
Indeed, recent scholarship by Carole Spencer traces a direct lineage between the
first Friends, the Quietists and Holiness Friends (2004). Spencer claims eight key
characteristics to early Quaker theology in terms of its emphasis on Scripture,
eschatology, conversion, charisma, evangelism, suffering, mysticism and perfection. Early Quakerism was its own distinct kind of holiness movement. Whilst no
subsequent Quaker tradition has encompassed all eight in the same way, the
Holiness Friends of the nineteenth century come the closest. Only the outward
liturgical form changed, she argues (Spencer, 2004).

What had also changed was the understanding of time but this change had taken place at the end of the seventeenth century. Evangelical Friends adopted sabbatarianism and exchanged the Day of the Lord for the Lord's Day. This may suggest a weakening of the intimacy with God that early Friends had found so vital, although many Holiness Friends also claimed dramatic transforming experiences of God's power in their lives. In short, the evangelical liturgical reform merely swapped the peculiarities for programming as the means to meantime obedience, but stopped short of fuller liturgical reform.

For other Gurneyite Friends, particularly those of the Holiness tendency, only the ordinances now separated them from their Protestant counterparts and some, led by David Updegraff, began in the 1880s to campaign for the possibility of water baptism. Most Yearly Meetings maintained the traditional Quaker line against outward baptism and in 1887, the Richmond 'Declaration of Faith', endorsed by most Gurneyite Yearly Meetings, offered clear guidance:

> We reverently believe that, as there is one Lord and one faith, so there is, under the Christian dispensation, but one baptism (Ephesians 4:4–5), even that whereby all believers are baptized in the one spirit into the one body (1 Corinthians 12:13 RV). This is not an outward baptism with water, but a spiritual experience; not the putting away of the filth of the flesh (1 Peter 3:21), but that inward work which, by transforming the heart and settling the soul upon Christ, brings forth the answer of a good conscience towards God, by the resurrection of Jesus Christ, in the experience of his love and power, as the risen and ascended Savior. No baptism in outward water can satisfy the description of the apostle, of being buried with Christ by baptism unto death (Romans 6:4). It is with the Spirit alone that any can thus be baptized. In this experience, the announcement of the forerunner of our Lord is fulfilled, 'He shall baptize you with the Holy Ghost and with fire' (Matthew 3:11).
>
> ('Declaration of Faith ...', 1887)

The 'Declaration' continues, after Barclay and Gurney, that the Great Commission of Matthew 28:18–20 was not designed to set up a new ritual. In this way, Paul could claim in 1 Corinthians 1:17 that he had come to preach, not to baptise. When the Great Commission talks of making disciples of all nations and baptising them, it is connected with the spiritual power released at Pentecost, not with an outward form.

Updegraff continued to seek toleration but found it only within his own Yearly Meeting in Ohio. When the other Gurneyite Yearly Meetings formed Five Years Meeting, later Friends United Meeting, to coordinate common concerns such as mission and education work, Ohio remained outside the body. This Yearly Meeting was later to become Eastern Region of Evangelical Friends International, a separate umbrella group for Yearly Meetings either more Holiness or more conservative in disposition.

The other Evangelical schismatics of the nineteenth century were the Wilburites of the 1840s and 1850s and then those who broke away in the 1870s and 1880s over the increasing influence of revivalism and the advent of pastoral Quakerism:

'Innovation became a scornful or pathetic invective among them' (Taber, 1978, p. 76), whilst 'the hedge' remained an important testimony. The Meeting for Worship remained the least changed aspect of this form of Quakerism and vocal ministry was given in the context of Quietistic concerns over speaking only out of obedience to the Inward Guide, the Living Christ, rather than an 'unhallowed' breaking of the silence (ibid., p. 78). Taber states that because these Friends saw Christ as the head of the Church, the sole purpose of worship was to be ' "in a condition" in which his Spirit could truly guide the whole meeting' (ibid., p. 80). Following that guidance might involve prayer, praise, teaching, preaching, or continued inward communion. Traditionally but not necessarily, prayers were the first and last vocal contributions.

Taber suggests that the experience of worship was akin to entering a different realm, of consciousness for those who had already experienced a baptism of the Spirit (ibid., p. 81). This baptism might occur during private devotions, in Meeting, or during 'an opportunity', a meeting for worship between a Minister and one other person or a family. Worship was to take participants to Christ and leave them there.

The Wilburite and Conservative Yearly Meetings of the nineteenth century were joined in 1905 by North Carolina made up of Monthly Meetings who opposed the imposition of a uniform discipline by the Yearly Meeting. Whilst these groups broke away with Gurneyite Quakerism for a range of reasons, they found unity as the Conservative branch. Numbers have dwindled and the seven Yearly Meetings are now three: Ohio, Iowa and North Carolina (with a group in Canada linked to a new Conservative British Yearly Meeting, the Friends in Christ). These Meetings have maintained a Christocentric unprogrammed worship in which the Inward Light is still a central concept and, as in Barclay, revelation has a higher authority than Scripture, but is confirmed by Scripture: 'Historically, Conservative Quakerism can best be understood as a defense of that precious inward place where the Living Christ, the Seed, the Life, the Light leading to God could meet with the individual worshipper as well as with the gathered meeting' (Taber, 1978, p. 75).

Until as late as the 1940s, it would be possible to hear ministry in the Quietistic nasal sing-song intonation (ibid., p. 76). Even today, some Conservatives still use the plain speech and adopt plain dress. We return to them in Chapter 6. Next, we consider the Modernist tendency within Quakerism, how it constructed Liberal Quakerism at the beginning of the twentieth century (replacing Evangelical Quakerism in Britain and harnessing Hicksite and Beanite tendencies in the US), and became dominant within the Gurneyite Yearly Meetings within Five Years Meeting by 1907.

The architects of the Liberal Quakerism that emerged at the end of the nineteenth century were all Modernist Evangelicals, Friends whose dedication to modernism and its consequences was to undermine their evangelicalism. In the United States, Rufus Jones became the prime mover for a Quakerism keenly aware of itself as part of the mystical tradition within Christianity, one more relevant to its age, more open to its own diversity and the world it sat within, and one dedicated to social witness. He was converted to this vision by the British Friend, John Wilhelm Rowntree, when they met each other in Switzerland in 1897.

In Britain, the freedoms the Evangelicals had won and the consequent lowering of the hedge ironically was to undo their dominance within the Yearly Meeting. Less likely to separate into different groups as one bound by a smaller scale of geography and greater bonds of kinship than their American counterparts, British Quakerism underwent a difficult and contested transition in the final decades of the nineteenth century.

The effects of Darwinian thinking and of higher criticism within biblical scholarship were to slowly infiltrate a group who had come to place Scripture as primary, albeit within an unprogrammed tradition, that is, a form which is predicated on some idea of encounter. Rather than continue the Evangelical reaction to the Enlightenment, that faith and reason were separate spheres, there were suggestions that Quakers could instead adopt a reasonable faith. This 'new thinking' was given a public Quaker platform at a conference in Manchester in 1895 and encouraged by a succession of Summer Schools in the years that followed.

Rufus Jones, already editor of *The American Friend*, took it in a Modernist direction after meeting with Rowntree on 1897. In the early years of the twentieth century Jones took on the Holiness Friends directly and secured a Modernist victory within Five Years Meeting (the umbrella body for Gurneyite Yearly Meetings) in 1907 (Hamm, 1988, p. 172). He also attended Hicksite Quaker gatherings and through social justice work, began a path of cooperation that would eventually lead to some Yearly Meetings reuniting in the 1940s and 1950s.

The Hicksites were by this stage, according to Geoffrey Kaiser (1994), more accurately described as Beanite. Joel and Hannah Bean were Gurneyites from Iowa originally. They supported the Evangelicalism of the 1860s and 1870s (Wood, 1978, p. 65) but became more wary of the revival influence as the silence became anachronistic to so many. They came head to head with the visiting David Updegraff in their own Yearly Meeting in 1888 and felt marginalised by the Yearly Meeting's enthusiastic response to Updegraff (Hamm, 1988, p. 139). They moved to California, at that time part of the Iowa Yearly Meeting, but continued to struggle with the revivalist tendencies. In response, they built a small Meeting House at College Park. They adopted a modernist statement of faith emphasising the headship of the Holy Spirit, the reality of the Living Christ, the free ministry, the testimony to simplicity, and responsible citizenship (Kaiser, 1994). Kaiser argues that these five points equally characterised the Quakerism of Hicksite Yearly Meetings as they entered the Twentieth Century. Worship was held on the basis of silence, the formulation of Beanite and Hicksite Quakerism essentially Modernist, that is, committed to a post-millennial vision of social justice as part of a faith open to the world and relevant to the age.

Jones and Rowntree and William Charles Braithwaite collaborated on plans for a multi-volume history of Quakerism. Their vision was both to open Quakerism up to the world and enable it to retain its distinctive identity. History was seen as a key tool to secure a sense of difference (Hamm, 1988, p. 155). In Britain, Quakers had only become full citizens, able to join the professions or attend any university without doctrinal compromise in 1870 and, coupled with the excitement about the new thinking, the years 1895–1910 have been called the 'Quaker renaissance' (Kennedy, 2001). It was a period of energy and pride in creating and reflecting on this latest version of the Quaker tradition (Phillips, 1989).

The authority of Scripture was diminished, as it had been by the worldly scholarship these Friends followed, in the new vision and Jones in particular presented Quakerism as part of the mystical tradition (Braithwaite, 1912, Introduction). In brief, this new 'Liberal Quakerism' was based on four main characteristics, modernist in outlook but also specifically different. The first was that experience, not Scripture, was primary, and gave authority for belief and action. The second was that faith needed to be relevant to the age. Quakerism was not again to be stuck with anachronistic peculiarities or indeed an intellectually suspect dependence on Scripture. Third, given the second, Friends were to be open to new Light from whatever quarter it may come. Fourth, these Quakers adopted the idea of progressivism, the belief that new revelation had greater authority than old (an idea Isichei first identifies within Quakerism in 1874 – 1970, p. 34).

Early Friends had placed revelation as having greater authority than Scripture but claimed that all revelation was confirmed by Scripture. This was echoed by Barclay. Evangelicals had placed Scripture as primary and some had mistrusted the idea of unmediated revelation. The Liberals placed revelation as primary, and also as sufficient. In other words, there was no necessary confirming role for Scripture. Jones and Rowntree and the Liberal Friends of the early twentieth century were clearly Christian. However, the combination of these four characteristics with their emphasis on experience and continuing revelation gave this version of Quakerism an unprecedented freedom for change. Indeed, given these characteristics, there was no theological place that this Quakerism needed to be tied to or to return to. It was not tied to Scripture, or any text, or even to tradition. (Modernist Gurneyism followed a similar list of characteristics but qualified experience as being 'spiritual experience' and the Light, 'the Light of Christ'. Indeed all twentieth-century Quaker Evangelicalism would be influenced by this modernist thinking, except that Scripture was still required to confirm revelation.)

Each century brings its own crucibles of change, whether the debates of how reformed the Church could be in the seventeenth century, or the revivals of the eighteenth and nineteenth century. The challenges to tradition in the twentieth century came from secularisation and from the increasing attempts to make God plausible and reasonable in the face of so much war and the Holocaust.

Within a rationalist tradition consciously open to 'new Light', untied to any particular text or tradition, it was inevitable that Liberal Quaker believing would become pluralistic. In 1921, the section on Christian Doctrine in the British 'book of discipline' (the key authoritative text for Friends) was replaced with a section entitled 'Illustrative Spiritual Experiences of Friends'. As early as 1930, Jones was asked whether it is necessary to be a Christian to be a Quaker. Belief became personal, rather than prescribed. Through the 1950s, 1960s and 1970s, Liberal Quaker belief diversified. In 1966, draft membership regulations were rejected by Yearly Meeting as being too prescriptively Christian. In 1980, Janet Scott, in her Swarthmore Lecture, the annual lecture of Britain Yearly Meeting, set out a Quaker theology. Faced with the question as to whether Quakers needed to be Christian, she wrote, 'Thus we may answer the question "Are Quakers Christian?" by saying that it does not matter. What matters to Quakers is not the label by which we are called or call ourselves, but the life' (Scott, 1980, p. 70). In the early 1990s, there were Hindu Quakers, Buddhist Quakers, Muslim Quakers and even a Moonie Quaker present within British Quakerism.

This had become possible through two distinct mechanisms. The first was the continuing value given silence within worship, and the parallel demotion of the value of words. We will look at this further in Chapter 6. Combined with the diversification and a cultural secularisation, it meant that ministry in Meeting may say very little which was explicitly religious and give very little clue as to what might be acceptable or normative Quaker theology. In this way, belief and changing patterns of belief were often invisible and faith transmission was weakened.

The second mechanism is that belief itself as a category was marginalised. The wariness over theology and the idea that words could not ever adequately describe religious experience contributed to the creation of a form of Quakerism which became defined not by belief but by behaviour. Thus, the form of worship became separated from any necessary form of accompanying theology, other than the belief that silence itself was theologically valid.

In this way, Liberal Quakerism came to operate a system of a 'double culture'. In terms of believing, Liberal Quakerism was permissive, always open to new light and based in the ongoing interpretation of experience. In terms of form, for example, its method of worship, Liberal Quakerism was conformist and conservative. In a group that places so much emphasis on continuing revelation and on seeking, there are always some who grieve for what has gone before. Certainly, as Liberal Quakerism liberalised and became post-Christian (in terms of the numbers of those using non-Christian language within the group) (Dandelion, P., 1996, p. 165), some grieved the pluralism. In terms of group cohesion, however, using the form as glue was as effective as using doctrine. Maintaining the historic testimony against creeds, these Quakers simply adopted a behavioural creed (that is, a credal attitude to the way in which the group is to be religious) instead, echoing the codification of practice of the Quietists.

However, there are key differences between the behavioural codes of the Quietists and of 'liberal-Liberal' Friends. Following the abolition of the

Liberal Belief Culture (that is, Belief)	**Behavioural Creed** (Form)
Non-credal	Credal
Religious basis	Pragmatic basis
Individually decided	Collectively agreed
Individually held	Collectively operated
Open to individual reinterpretation	Collectively changed
Accommodates diversity	Requires conformity
Diversity between participants	Commonality of practice
Inclusivist	Exclusivist
Syncretic	Conservative
Permissive	Conformist
Change of paradigm in last thirty years	Basically unchanged for 350 years
No official control	Official control (for example, Clerks and Elders)
Unofficial leadership ('weighty Friends')	Rule-defined (book of discipline)
Not discussed often	Discussed frequently
Not required for Membership	Required for Membership
Not central to perceived meaning of Quakerism	Central identification with Quaker identity
Subordinate	Dominant
Does not function as a framework	Meta-narrative

Figure 4.3 The Quaker double culture (Dandelion, P., 1996, p. 131)

peculiarities in the 1860s, Friends had been able to be invisible on the street and maintain a mixed-religion household without fear of disownment. In time, home visits by Elders would decrease and by the late twentieth century, Meetings felt it increasingly inappropriate to pass judgement on anything that happened outside of the Meeting House (Dandelion, P., 1996, p. xxvi). It became up to individuals to decide what and when to share elements of their life outside of Meeting. In this way, the behavioural creed of the Liberals is confined to the Meeting House:

'Quaker time', the time explicitly spent as a Quaker can also be confined in this way, with some members attending only rarely.

In other words, the outward markers of the codes are minimal and are confined to the Meeting House. They need not affect consumption in the way they did for Quietist Friends and their management need last no longer than an hour on Sunday morning (worship time was reduced again in the twentieth century). The codes are not concerned with marking off a peculiar or separated people over and against the world. Indeed, what constitutes 'the world' is small and, indeed, may vary from Friend to Friend. Public Quaker statements against, for example, the state lottery, or war highlight the few ways in which most Friends would find themselves peculiar. Rather, the codes are about enshrining cohesion and conformity about those elements of the Quaker life now deemed definitional. If a liberal-Liberal Quaker is asked what Quakers believe, s/he is likely to answer in terms of not having priests, sacraments, hymns, etc. It seems as if the question is being evaded but the Friend is merely answering the question about what defines this branch of Quakerism. It is not what Quakers believe that matters but the way in which the group is religious.

None of the four basic Liberal Quaker characteristics specified a belief-content. Rather, they define a common approach to the religious enterprise. It is this approach, accommodated through unprogrammed worship, which defines Liberal Quakerism. Critically, those given responsibility such as Elders, have their authority clearly limited to matters of form. Elders, for example, manage the silence of worship, deciding when to end worship and interrupting over-long

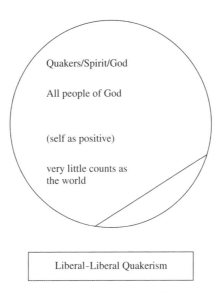

Quakers/Spirit/God

All people of God

(self as positive)

very little counts as the world

Liberal-Liberal Quakerism

Figure 4.4 Liberal-Liberal Quaker understandings of 'the world'

ministry. They are not, however, given the authority to police the content of ministry (Dandelion, P., 1996, pp. 207–11).

The adherence to form appears paradoxical given the permissive attitude afforded other parts of Quakerism and the desire to be as inclusive as possible. However, in a few larger Meetings, there is now regular semi-programmed all-age worship. In these situations, perhaps monthly, a theme is set for the Meetings and people come prepared with contributions. The children stay in the Meeting House and the worship is designed to be inclusive. This innovation is on a different scale from the less visible individuation of belief but it does highlight the possibility of change. However, until there is a whole range of worship options, or people are worshipping alone at home in their own way, the 'glue' of the behavioural creed remains in place and silence remains the basis of worship.

Thus, in terms of worship practice, Liberal Friends are not inclusive but are clear about the value of silence. No longer the sole true Church, they need no longer offer salvation for everybody. If unprogrammed worship doesn't suit the enquirers, they can find an equally legitimate liturgy elsewhere. This attitude is illustrated well in the British Quaker responses to the World Council of Churches exercise in the 1980s on baptism, eucharist and the ministry.

In 1905, in the shadow of the Welsh revival, an article in *The British Friend* paid tribute to 'the Power of Silence', claiming that 'when the Divine presence was most strongly felt, it was accompanied not by fervent prayers or songs or words of any kind, but by the touch of a heavenly stillness that made words unnecessary' (*The British Friend*, June 1905, p. 147). Here, British Friends celebrated the silence over and against other liturgical forms.

In 1986, on baptism, British Friends maintained the historic rejection of water-baptism in their formal response to the World Council of Churches document, *Baptism, Eucharist and the Ministry* (1982). First, it was not a necessary inference from Scripture, but additionally they claimed that no one single rite could mark what was for them a continual process of growth in the Holy Spirit (*To Lima with Love*, 1986, p. 8). Interestingly, the Quaker response acknowledged that the grace of God is experienced by many through the outward rite of baptism (ibid.).

On eucharist, the Quakers claimed they shared many of the spiritual aspirations listed as aims of this central liturgical rite and again recognised that 'the words and symbolic actions of the eucharist are experienced by very many Christians as a most powerful means of grace, a grace which shines forth in their lives' (ibid., 1986, p. 9):

> In silence, without rite or symbol, we have known the Spirit of Christ so convincingly present in our quiet meetings that his grace dispels our faithfulness, our unwillingness, our fears, and sets our hearts aflame with the joy of adoration. We have thus felt the power of the Spirit renewing and recreating our love and friendship for all our fellows. This is our eucharist and this is our communion.
>
> (part of the Epistle from London Yearly Meeting 1928,
> as in *Quaker Faith and Practice*, 1995, 26.15)

The Quaker response argues that the validity of worship lies not in its form but in its power, and that worship without outward rite and symbol 'may equally serve as a channel' for God's power and grace. Christ's invitation to remembrance is not to be limited to formal worship and that 'separating a particular sacrament and making it a focal point in worship can obscure the sacramental validity of the rest of creation and of human life' (*To Lima with Love*, 1986, p. 10).

These points are echoed by the extracts selected for the section on 'Sacraments' in the 1994 book of discipline. The book of Revelation is not evident and instead of the assertion of a singular position on the truth of the matter, these present-day Friends claim an equivalence for their liturgical form:

> We do not say that to observe the sacraments is wrong, but that such observance is not essential to wholehearted Christian discipleship and the full Christian experience. We do not judge our fellow Christians to whom the outward sacraments mean so much. Rather do we wish, by prayerful fellowship with them, to be led unitedly with them to a deeper understanding of what underlies those sacraments, and so to share a richer experience of the mind of Christ.
>
> (*Quaker Faith and Practice*, 1995, 27.39)

Is this the meantime position of a group seeing itself as a part of the true church? Bria writes from his Orthodox perspective:

> The eucharist represents our redemption in Jesus Christ and its conclusion in the coming of the Holy Spirit on the church. But it is not just a commemorative festival; the eucharistic liturgy 'actualizes' the redemptive ministry of Jesus Christ in sharing his own body and blood with the baptized faithful. The body and blood of Christ are the true food and drink of the church, and the role of the eucharistic liturgy is to create, nurture and sustain the *koinonia* of the church.
>
> (Bria, 1996, p. 1)

At one level, it seems reasonable that Friends, having lost their sense of imminent endtime, should see all meantime forms as equally legitimate meantime choices. However, if Liberal Friends are claiming an equivalence for their liturgical form, it is of an alternative ordering. It may be an equivalent channel for God's grace, love and power, even for fellowship in the Holy Spirit, but it is no longer described in the same terms as those in the churches describe the eucharist. The latest British Quaker book of discipline contains no entries on redemption, or atonement. The remembrance which John Luffe had no need of, 'for Christ is about me and in me and [I] therefore cannot choose but remember him continually' (Braithwaite, 1912, p. 425), may still be irrelevant for Quakers of today, but perhaps for different reasons, that is, that they have nothing to remember. In terms of the place of liberal-Liberal Friends within our biblical understanding of time, most of them have left the chart and are operating by a different map.

Post-Christian Quakers and those of other faiths cannot subscribe to this Pauline map, given their theology. Without a First Coming, a Second one makes little

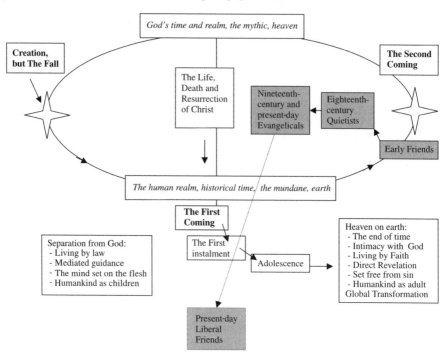

Figure 4.5 Liberal Quakers and the biblical understanding of time

sense. If the first Friends heard the alarm clock of the Second Coming ringing, if the Quietists pressed the 'snooze' button, and the Evangelicals turned the hands back a little, it seems as if most Liberals have removed the batteries or thrown the clock away.

However, some Liberal Friends disagree. Faced with the analysis of the first Friends here, there are a number of options. The first is that early Friends, if they were talking about the unfolding and soon-coming Second Coming (and John Punshon for one disagrees that they were anyway – 2001, p. 310), got it wrong. For example, it could be that they mistook the experience of the new inward covenant with God, as described by Barclay and Gurney and Punshon later and prefigured in Jeremiah 31:31–4 and Revelation 3:20, as the sign of the imminent Second Coming. Second, the first Friends may have got it right but humanity was not ready to accept God's invitation. This is a view informally suggested by Douglas Gwyn and suggests that the endtimes are invitational.

Third, Barclay and Gurney were wrong in their reading of experience and the Second Coming is indeed unfolding but not with the speed suggested by Paul's letters, but, perhaps, in God's time. In other words, and some Liberal Friends have suggested this to me, the Second Coming was unfolding for the first Friends and is still unfolding. In other words, Friends are still living a realising eschatology. Ferner Nuhn claims this has always been the Quaker position and calls it the 'eternal now' (Nuhn, 1981, p. 35). He claims Pentecost is the condition and initiation of the coming endtimes. Some post-millennial Evangelicals agree. The 'day of visitation' is an encounter with the risen Christ, a personal Pentecost, an individual eschatological experience as part of the ongoing formation of the Holy Nation and the ongoing Lamb's War: Jack Kirk has written 'that the experience of Pentecost is to be repeated in each generation' (1978, p. 89).

This view in either its Liberal or Evangelical versions brings with it complications, especially given the attitude of equivalence cited above in regard to different liturgical forms. Either the early Quaker insights regarding liturgical form which have been presented here as consequential to a particular sense of the endtimes are optional, or not. If not, it means that the unprogrammed way is still the legitimate and authentic mode of worship in these endtimes. In this case, the ecumenical position of Friends is tricky. Either, the unfolding endtimes are available to all and other Churches should cease from their anachronistic practices if they are to be faithful, or only a certain portion of God's people have this experience of the unfolding endtimes as yet, and those outside the vanguard can maintain their forms for the time being. Evangelical Friends can look to the ecumenical flavour of Barclay and Gurney and the weight they give a sincere heart in the context of their liturgical preferences. Few if any Liberal Friends, I suggest, would take either of these positions seriously. Rather, their version of the Second Coming, if they have one, is different from the biblical one, both in style and in consequences.

Liberal Friends then have also abandoned the sense of unfolding endtimes as experienced by the first Friends. Indeed, no group of Quakers in the world today sustains those claims. Barclay reinterpreted the emphasis of the radical liturgy of the 1650s in terms of a new covenant made possible through the First Coming, an inwardly intimate meantime and this has been followed by all traditions since, in various liturgical formats, until the liberal-Liberal construction of Quakerism. Here, the nature of intimacy and the existence of meantime has been brought into question, a theme we will pick up again in Chapter 7.

The next chapter looks more closely at the present-day practice of worship in Evangelical, Conservative and Liberal settings.

CHAPTER 5

Present-Day Practice

Quakers throughout the world today can be divided between those who maintain an unprogrammed form of worship and those who express their unmediated relationship with God through some level of programming. The latter group is the majority, including the large groups of Friends in East Africa, South America, and most of the United States of America.

Programmed Friends world-wide are connected with either Friends United Meeting, Evangelical Friends International, or are unaffiliated/independent. Friends United Meeting had its roots in the modernist Gurneyite tendency, Evangelical Friends International in the holiness/revivalist one. However, both were influenced by Fundamentalism in the twentieth century and the range of theological opinions within both groupings overlap. If anything, Evangelical Friends International comprise those Meetings that have historically adopted more holiness or more conservative positions.

Unprogrammed Friends are divided between the Liberal and Conservative traditions. The Liberal Yearly Meetings do not have the same kind of umbrella bodies as the Evangelical ones. In the United States, Friends General Conference acts as a service agency to the many Liberal Yearly Meetings that subscribe to it, but all Liberal Yearly Meetings are independent.

The Conservative Yearly Meetings meet in association with each other but are also independent of each other. There are three in the United States and one bridging Conservative Friends in Britain and Canada (who originally emigrated from Britain). Ohio Yearly Meeting (Conservative) maintains an associate membership scheme that allows sympathetic Friends world-wide to affiliate, even whilst retaining membership in another Yearly Meeting.

None of the above groups claim a sense of an imminent Second Coming,

What follows is a limited attempt to try and understand how the different theological bases that we have considered in the last chapter play out in everyday settings. Data from fieldwork at an Evangelical Friends Church in Northwest Yearly Meeting in 2003 is set alongside data drawn from North Carolina Conservative Yearly Meeting and data collected in Britain.

The Evangelical Friends Church

The church in this case study is part of Northwest Yearly Meeting. Originally Oregon Yearly Meeting until 1971, it was established in 1893. The Yearly Meeting broke away from Five Years Meeting (FYM, now Friends United Meeting) in 1926, concerned at the degree of doctrinal liberty within FYM and their desire that the Richmond 'Declaration of Faith' serve as a doctrinal basis for FYM. The Yearly Meeting was part of the Association of Evangelical Friends when it began in 1947, which became Evangelical Friends Alliance in 1965, and then Evangelical Friends International in 1989. Missionary work has been particularly active in Bolivia and Peru, although also in the Phillipines, Taiwan, Burundi, Rwanda, Mexico and India. The Yearly Meeting has a membership of about seven thousand.

In the 'Friends Faith – what Friends believe' section of the book of discipline of Northwest Yearly Meeting, there are sub-sections on 'The Baptism with the Holy Spirit', 'God's Kingdom', 'The Spiritual Experience' and 'Worship' amongst others (*Faith and Practice*, 1998, p. 6). We will consider these short passages in turn as they refer to our main themes of time and intimacy, of the inward and the outward. On baptism, we read:

> We believe Christ's baptism to be the inward receiving of the promised Holy Spirit, whereby the believer is immersed in Jesus' power, purity, and wisdom. This baptism is the essential Christian baptism: an experience of cleansing from sin that supplants old covenant rituals. The sanctification that is initiated with this experience is a continuing work of the Holy Spirit in which we are instructed into righteous living and perfected in love ... (Ibid.)

On God's Kingdom:

> We believe the Church is called to demonstrate in this life the righteous character of God's present and coming Kingdom. The Kingdom is present now to the extent that the people of God hear His voice and obey it. The coming Kingdom will be initiated by the second appearing of Jesus Christ (as foretold by the prophets) and by the resurrection of the dead. The world will then be judged righteously by Jesus Christ and there will come everlasting punishment for the finally unrepentant wicked and everlasting blessedness for the righteous. At that time, the world will be freed from the grip of evil and satanic power, and Christ will reign over a restored universe (Ibid.).

This is clearly meantime theology in line with the Richmond Declaration examined in Chapter 4 above. What is interesting is that whilst baptism is still spiritualised and internalised, the section on the Second Coming can be read in terms of the expectation of an outward reappearance. The passage is not explicit either way. The section on 'The Spiritual Experience' follows:

> We believe that we may experience Christ directly and immediately without the necessity of priestly or ceremonial intervention and that this experience is available to every person. The spiritual life is nourished by the Holy Spirit, who teaches and guides us both individually and corporately according to His commandments. For Friends the supper of the Lord is an inward feeding on Christ by faith in response to his broken body and shed blood. (Ibid.)

In this way, worship is seen to be without formal liturgy, rite, or ceremony. Rather, everything points towards the inward intimacy with God, framed within a Scriptural understanding. We can see here Spencer's contention that this form of Quakerism is little different from Quietism, or even the first Friends, save in outward form (2004). This understanding of worship is highlighted in the 'Worship' section.

> Worship is the adoring response of heart and mind to the Spirit of God. The meeting for worship brings a personal and corporate renewal, and edification and communion of believers, and a witness of the Gospel to the unconverted. We recognise the value of silence to center our thoughts upon God. We believe the Spirit speaks to worshipers through persons He has prepared and selected, whose message may be given in various modes by men or women, children or adults. We believe God calls some persons to a special preaching ministry, which the church should respectfully receive. Friends observe the first day of the week for corporate worship and rest. (Ibid.)

The church building was built in the 1960s and replaced a downtown neighbourhood Friends church. The modern building is clearly a church, a cross extending skywards from the raised centre of its roof, almost forming a spire. This raised section has stained glass on its vertical faces and coloured light falls down inside the church. Inside, the worship area called 'the Sanctuary' is separated from the hall by a partition that is largely glass, allowing activity on the other side to be viewed easily. Latecomers can see where the service has reached, or those waiting to enter at the beginning of the service can see when the music rehearsals are over. The partition both separates and includes, drawing those in the hall area in towards the centre of the liturgical action, breaking down the separation between formal worship and informal community. This contrasts with the outer walls of the church that are a combination of brick and stained glass, giving no particular clue as to what lies within. Church members once inside are separated from the world. They can don their name-tags without embarrassment and reveal their hopes and fears in prayers and praise removed from everyday life. It is not particularly well-lit by natural light, unlike some of the modern unprogrammed Meeting Houses (one in Texas has a roof which opens literally to the sky), but the enclosed nature of the internal space is a shared feature of most churches (and cf. Matt. 6:6).

In the foyer area, there are pictures of missionary families and the invitation to pray for them and their work. Tapes of sermons of previous weeks, and copies of the church newsletter are on sale. A leaflet on Friends worship available to the newcomer reads in part:

> At the heart of vital Quakerism lies the experience of worship. When we worship we receive God's love for us and express our love for God ... For most groups of Quakers the *goal* of worship is the same, but the way it is done may vary. Some groups adhere to the practice of waiting in silence before the Present Christ, believing that any attempt to predetermine how the Spirit will lead may hinder the Spirit's working. Here the practice of 'centering' one's mind on Christ's Spirit within provides

refreshment as the words of the psalmist come to life, 'Be still and know that I am God.'(Psalm 46:10) And the prophet points to the source of empowerment. 'In quietness and trust is your strength.' (Isa. 30:15)

Other Friends acknowledge that lack of format does not insure inspired worship. They believe that the Spirit may also lead in the planning of the service, and that the order of service should be able to be laid down if the Spirit dictates. During the service, the focus is not on the leaders of worship, but on the Present Lord. It is totally opposite to an audience appreciating a performance, because *all* are involved in the act of worshiping God. Worship without participation is a contradiction of terms.

(Anderson, n.d)

The leaflet ends with a passage from the Richmond 'Declaration of Faith':

Worship is not an agenda of hymns to be sung and things to be said any more than the Church of Jesus Christ is a building of brick and stone. Worship is the loving interaction between God and the people of God who *are* the Church. It may be aided by format but is not to be confused with nor dependent on it. 'Worship is the adoring response of the heart and mind to the influence of the Spirit of God. It stands neither in forms nor in the formal disuse of forms ... it must be in Spirit and in truth (John 4:24).' (Ibid.)

Benches form a semi-circle around the stage, which is set up with a lectern placed centrally, a piano, various microphones for various parts of the service, and four chairs for those leading the worship, for example, three Pastors, or two and the visitor giving the message, and the 'worship leader', one of the four 'Ministers of Music'. There are three Pastors in this church, as well as a youth co-ordinator and the Ministers of Music. Four staff are employed in support roles. The newsletter shows that attendance is regularly about one hundred but that it has dropped in recent years. People sit throughout the worship area, with concentrations at the edges. On the backs of the benches are pockets for Bibles and hymnals.

An optional ten-minute silent worship precedes the start of the service, entitled 'Preparation for Worship'. Sometimes the doors to the sanctuary are left open in this time and greetings and conversation are audible and/or carry on within the Sanctuary within this time. Even people arriving further on in the Meeting may greet each other vocally and the atmosphere is relaxed. People dress smartly (if not in Sunday best, then in Sunday-better), but not formally.

'Meeting for Worship' lasts 75 minutes and typically comprises: a musical 'prelude'; opening words of welcome from one of the Pastors; a hymn; welcomes, announcements and prayers for those in need ('we know these things are in God's hands but ...') and including a prayer for the person giving 'the message', that they may be given the words 'you want us to hear'; the narrative – a reading or, for example, a dramatic interpretation of a scriptural passage; music to accompany the offertory; 'choruses' (less formal than the hymn with repeated sections as led by the 'worship leader'); the message, lasting around fifteen minutes; up to fifteen minutes of 'open worship' ('Communion after the Manner of Friends'); prior to closing music and closing words from one of the Pastors. Children are invited to leave before the message. 'Friendship Pads' are passed around early in worship and all present give their name and whether they are visiting or a member or want further contact. Elders are available to talk with after worship.

This liturgical form is clearly self-identified as Quaker and one respondent claimed that the church and its Yearly Meeting were the most 'conservative' (in terms of conserving Quakerism) within Evangelical Friends International. The church describes itself as a Friends Church and as a 'Christ-Centered Quaker Community of Ministers' and the service is called 'Meeting for Worship'. The 'open worship' to which the rest of the service points, is described as 'communion after the manner of Friends' in terms of it offering that unmediated and inward access with Christ and God as described in Revelation 3:20. The church does not practice water baptism. The ministry team is made up of Pastors, not priests, and all are described as ministers. In other ways, the liturgy is a meantime one. On one Sunday, the hymn 'On Higher Ground' looked forward to the coming of the Kingdom, one of the choruses, 'Soon and Very Soon' included the words 'Soon and very soon, we are going to see the King.' The theme of hope was referred to several times as being concerned with the coming of the Kingdom. The service reflected both a sense of Christ's presence and a sense of future prospect. It was a perfect hybrid of Quaker distinctive and strategic meantime practice. The only elements that differed from Barclay and Gurney were the degree of pre-programming and the length of open worship.

The open worship followed the message. On one occasion, a woman came to the front, to the 'altar rail' in an electric wheelchair and asked for prayers for her forthcoming time in hospital. I wondered if she had chosen this moment rather than the earlier call for prayers to avoid direct attention, but on hearing her request, two Pastors rose from their chairs and went to her, and laid their hands on her, inviting anyone else who wanted to pray with them. About fifteen people left their seats and moved towards the women, either touching her directly or via the touch of another. The woman's muffled voice could be heard from within the huddle of people standing over her explaining what was happening for her, and then one of the Pastors led a prayer that could be heard by everyone. Then people returned to their seats, and the open worship continued as before with two more ministries in the remaining minutes. This particular church may have the longest period of open worship in the Yearly Meeting. Elsewhere too, the open worship may be more full of testimony, silence appearing as a sign of spiritual lethargy to those with Wesleyan holiness influences. As one informant said to me, each church needs to know how it is using the open worship and be clear about it.

In some way, the Pastors were behaving as Elders might in an unprogrammed meeting, acting spontaneously within a set of pre-agreed responsibilities. Their action differed from the rules of unprogrammed worship through their immediate response to, and interaction with, the ministry of another in a way that created activity. As we have noted, Elders' *public* roles in the unprogrammed traditions are usually confined to curtailment.

In term of the music or prayer, the Pastors modelled an emotional restraint. No hands were raised during the choruses and only a gentle swaying or foot-tapping was evident on stage. In the pews, couples held hands more during this part of the worship or stroked each other's backs, some held their hands out open in front of them, but nothing more explicit. Agreement with the prayers was voiced very softly: 'It is not outwardly emotional, yet tears and laughter sometimes break in as little touches from heaven' (Mylander, 1978, p. 124). Respondents were comfortable with the level of emotion as well as the level of freedom to respond to the music as they wished (although one recent recruit from the Pentecostal tradition talked of needing to remember to keep his 'hand down'). This contrasted with another Friends Church visited, less self-identified as Quaker and more consciously a community church, where emotional restraint was far less evident. In more Holiness churches, services might include an altar call. In Africa and South America, expressions of emotion are normative. (There too, worship is less restrained by the clock with less formal starting and ending times, depending partly on the needs of rural life.)

After worship and fifteen minutes' social time ('fellowship'), four or five different 'adult offerings' in Christian education took place for an hour in different parts of the extensive complex. The variety of classes available was given by one interviewee as an example of how this church was less anti-intellectual than some other Evangelical churches. It was claimed that the church had an Evangelical faith without an Evangelical culture. There is extended fellowship time after the classes. (In contrast to this timetable, a Meeting in Minnesota starts at 9 a.m. with an hour of unprogrammed worship, followed by a class, and then an hour of programmed worship. The programming usually consists of a hymn, thirty minutes' open worship, a speaker for ten to fifteen minutes, fifteen minutes' more silence, and a closing hymn. The speaker is normally a Member. There is no Pastor.)

Over the years, the spontaneous and informal worship of the Revival Meetings in the 1870s has become routinised in some ways. The format of the worship follows a familiar pattern even if it changes from week to week: one week, it was suggested, 'we haven't sung in a long time.' Most interviewees had come from other reformed churches and had found little different between those services and the one here. The open worship usually constitutes the main difference but also is one of the main draws. One Friend from a Roman Catholic background did find contrasts between those two groups but generally assumed all forms to be equivalent.

Interviews revealed that there were different views over preferred styles of music. The contemporary choruses are not liked by everyone. One respondent intimated that they lacked the 'craftsmanship' or design of more classical pieces but also that their tendency to the first-person singular and the emotional increased the focus on the individual. A sample chorus verse, illustrating this point, follows:

I want to know you, I want to hear your voice.
I want to know you more.
I want to touch you, I want to see your face.
I want to know you more.

(from 'In the Secret' by Andy Park, Mercy/Vineyard Publishing)

For this Friend, worship was necessarily a collective activity, a humbling adoration of God, an acknowledging of God, in which the music or form should transcend the individual composer or participant, space and time. One interviewee suggested 'theology is safer than emotion' meaning it is more likely to be authentic. David Martin refers to a 'demotic' understanding of music where the impact of the music is deemed to be of greater concern than its appropriateness (see also Chapter 6 below, on foot-stomping in the Liberal tradition), where the message is more important than the medium (2002, p. 49). Interestingly, he claims that such an approach to music sets up tension between preacher and music as they vie for both the right level of high and low liturgical emphasis and the maintenance of sincerity and charisma (ibid.). In this church, preferences for musical and pastoral preferences are also allowed to play out, given the choice on offer.

Other changes have taken place. The 'altar rails' (or as one Friend said, 'the rails on the stage') have been remodelled to be less prominent and were removed for a while, much to the dismay of many. One Friend claimed they came to church for the encouragement they received from meeting with their faith community and for accountability. Compared to a previous church this Friend had attended, the Friends had a different and shorter list of proscribed activity but also 'harangued' people less. Sermons were less about how to live on a daily basis or about what to avoid, for example, materialism. There was less about personal sacrifice and less testimony about what people had been previously hiding. However, at one time, a Friend would regularly stand in the opening worship and say that there was someone, they knew who they were, who needed to be held accountable. Then a person would stand up and move forward to the altar rail, accompanied by the speaker, and others would join them there in prayer. People would be praying and crying. Admonition and repentance were managed without naming the person who would voluntarily expose themselves, or the offence.

On another occasion, one Friend spoke during open worship of wishing to make a commitment to the church and came to the front and sat on the bench nearest the rails, where she was joined by a Pastor and another Friend in prayer.

Jack Kirk claims that being a Quaker Pastor is unlike being a Pastor in any Protestant church. The worship needs to be flexible to take account of the leadings of the Holy Spirit, the Pastor may not speak at all, everyone present needs to feel both responsibility and freedom (1978, p. 100):

By and large, Friends worship has a Protestant feel, but what distinguishes it is that the focus of the service is not the sermon, but the open worship – the period of silence that is sometimes very brief, but in some places takes up at least half the service ... it is an embodiment of Friends understanding of covenantal Christianity. The hymns and scriptures which surround it have one purpose only: to lead the meeting into a direct encounter with God.

(Punshon, 2001, p. 200)

As Punshon argues, 'Silence is still at the heart of the programmed meeting' (ibid., p. 195) and 'Silence is the most powerful symbol of our dependence on God' (ibid., p. 205). Where this is true for Evanglical Friends, they remain faithful to the Gurneyite sense of intimacy, what John Punshon calls the Quaker understanding of covenantal Christianity, based on Jeremiah 31:31–4. As Charles Mylander states, 'programming of itself does not hinder the Holy Spirit' (1978, p. 133). Rather, the Holy Spirit leads the preparation (ibid.): 'the goal of every meeting for worship is the evident presence and power of the Lord in the midst' (ibid., p. 124).

Respondents were clear that a succession of different Pastors had affected the structure and feel of worship very little. The Pastor, rather, sets the tone of worship. The only innovation had been the introduction of choruses. One interviewee noted the importance of the Ministers of Music in the shaping of the worship. Even in terms of sermons, respondents usually found something worthwhile in the message, regardless of the speaker; one interviewee claimed that she didn't have a favourite Pastor, all were 'spoken through'.

One respondent cited this collective responsibility as the biggest difference between Friends and his previous church, that it was the form that was different, not the experience. Respondents suggested that the open worship could be abused by people simply sharing their own emotions, or by coming with a pre-prepared message and standing early. The husband of one informant had lost faith in the unprogrammed form because 'people said dumb things'. Another felt that introducing discussions on interfaith dialogue, say, as a church activity, might not be helpful given this open format and the way confusion can be so easily aired.

All respondents mentioned the importance of educating newcomers clearly in what the silence was about. Care had been taken to get the words in 'the bulletin' (which gives and explains the order of service) right and a separate leaflet on unprogrammed worship and ministry had been provided. Those who had given ministry had been thanked for it. Those considering membership are offered an eight-week class held annually.

None of my interviewees wanted to see open worship dropped, even those who had experienced difficulty with it at first, and some wanted to see it lengthened or at least not closed by the clock. One Friend claimed any other part of the service could go, but not the open worship. One suggested having further unprogrammed worship at another time in the week. Its placement after the sermon was generally liked, giving participants a chance to reflect on the sermon. The music at the end of the worship was preferred to ending with notices, as used to happen, as a way of 'wrapping back up' to a more profane level.

The structure of the morning was generally appreciated. Fellowship time directly after worship is a recent innovation and if worship ran on, could lead to people arriving late for the classes, but as one Friend said 'the "hall classes" are important too.'

The open worship was not felt by interviewees to be seen as a superior means of worship. One had had the experience of needing to be re-baptised, fully immersed, on becoming a Baptist as his previous Methodist 'sprinkling' was considered inadequate by his new affiliation. In contrast, there was a story of a previous Pastor at this church offering a couple water-baptism in spite of the Quaker tradition and the Richmond 'Declaration of Faith' in the front of the Yearly Meeting's *Faith and Practice*.

Where there is no open worship, or where the worship is directed towards the sermon or communion, or where Scripture has become more important than the Living Word of Christ, then Friends have moved into a less traditionally Quaker place and may have dropped the sense of inward intimacy. These latter Friends may also be less distinctively sectarian in their presentation to the world, with a focus of being the community church rather than a particularly Quaker one. Some have dropped the term 'Friends' from their title. At a Yearly Meeting level, though, insights from Gurney and the Richmond 'Declaration of Faith' are maintained. In both these situations, Friends are working to be faithful in the meantime, with that sense of meantime coupled to a sense of inward intimacy working through and beyond outward forms, or not.

Friends in Evangelical Friends International Eastern Region and Southwest permit the outward ordinances (Punshon, 2001, p. 219). Gurney's tolerant ending to his affirmation of Quaker distinctiveness, that God 'is pleased to bless a variety of means to a variety of conditions' (1979, p. 168) allows this greater toleration. Gurney's Evangelical Christianity helped prepare Orthodox Friends to receive the revival of the 1860s but they ended up dropping his strong preference for worship based in silence, and, in these cases, dropping his reading of Scripture on the ordinances. However, his ecumenism, and sense of Quaker Christianity as just one part of the true Church makes even this move potentially legitimate. What becomes important is faithful and obedient waiting within a scriptural framework. Indeed, it is interesting that not more Friends Churches have adopted the outward ordinances in their own versions of their liturgical logic of equivalence (see Chapter 4).

Conservative Quaker Meeting

As previously mentioned, the Conservative tradition consists of Yearly Meetings which have broken away at different times and in different circumstances. Ohio was originally Wilburite, Iowa began as a reaction to Pastoral Quakerism, North Carolina (Conservative) reacted against Yearly Meeting attempts at uniformity, and the Friends in Christ started in Britain in 1993 as a reaction to the loss of Christianity amongst British Friends. At the same time, Ohio began the possibility of 'Affiliate membership' whereby Friends in other Yearly Meetings could also join Ohio. In Britain for example, some in sympathy with the Friends in Christ nevertheless retained their membership of Britain Yearly Meeting and joined Ohio as Affiliate members.

The section on worship in the Ohio book of discipline, unchanged in at least the last three revisions of 1968, 1977 and 1992, offers a description of worship. It includes:

> We meet together in silence and strive to free our minds and hearts for the purpose of spiritual worship. We must then wait in humble reverence for the spiritual ability to worship the Lord of Heaven and Earth in a manner acceptable to Him. As each soul feels a spirit of supplication answered by the quickening influence of the Holy Spirit, we approach the Throne of Grace, that is to say, we are enabled to enter into an attitude of true worship, in gratitude and praise. Though the nearness of God may result in spoken ministry or vocal prayer, the distinctive excellence of heavenly favor consists in the direct communication with the Heavenly Father by the inward revelation of the Spirit of Christ.
>
> *(The Book of Discipline of Ohio Yearly Meeting of the*
> *Religious Society of Friends*, 1992, p. 5)

Taber claims that Conservative Friends today have realised that preparation increases the chance of a 'favored' Meeting: preparation by each participant; preparation by those with gifts needed by the Meeting, for example, vocal ministry, eldering, and preparation of those who have experienced the inward baptism and who already know the 'gathered' silence and can slip into it more easily (1978, p. 84). Some may pray for the Meeting beforehand or have an acute sense of the spiritual state of the Meeting and be able to nurture the worshipping group within the worship and in the times between (ibid., p. 85). Daily Bible reading and worship time are still common amongst Conservative Friends. This advice on preparation is explicit in the Ohio Discipline as is advice on the teaching of children: 'Such should be taught, in proportion to their understanding, how to wait in stillness on the Lord, that they, too, may receive their portion of His spiritual favor through the tendering influence of His Holy Spirit' (*The Book of Discipline of Ohio Yearly Meeting*, 1992, p. 5).

A leaflet for visitors entitled 'Welcome to our Meeting' is more theologically explicit and is worth detailed examination. The quotation from Francis Howgill cited earlier at the end of Chapter 1 is on the cover. There is a general welcome prior to six sections on different aspects of Quaker faith and practice. The first section is entitled 'A Waiting Worship and a Free Gospel Ministry'. It begins:

> We gather in expectant silence to wait upon the Lord. When we gather in His name, Christ Jesus is truly here with us. Therefore we do not seek to worship, pray or sing in our own wisdom or strength, but to hear what the True Shepherd would have us do. The hour of worship is His, to program as He sees fit: our task is to respond with the worship, prayer, ministry, or song that He gives us.
>
> ('Welcome to our Meeting', n.d.)

This is similar to the Evangelical attitude towards their worship except that the Pastor has pre-programmed some of the worship under the leadership of the Holy Spirit, rather than that programming being given to the whole body during the time of worship. Following John 4:23–4, the leaflet makes this explicit: 'Since Christ Jesus is the head of the church, our worship should not depend on any one appointed person, but on Christ's living ministry in our midst'. There is also clarity that 'all true Gospel ministry is given by the direct prompting of Christ through his Holy Spirit'. Any true message is from the Lord and the speaker's accomplishments or feelings of unworthiness are irrelevant. The leaflet also encourages listening with a 'spiritual ear' so we may be 'richly nourished by a message that appears undistinguished in human terms: ' "Take no thought beforehand what ye shall speak ... but speak whatsoever shall be given you in that hour ... for it is not ye that speak but the Holy Ghost" – Mark 13:11' (ibid.). A dichotomy between the human and the divine is clear.

The leaflet continues that all are called to the ministry, men and women (Joel 2:28), and that none are paid for their ministry or appointed to fixed duties. The section ends with a passage from 1 Peter:

> As every man has received the gift, even so minister the same, one to another, as good stewards of the manifold grace of God. If any man speak, let him speak as the oracles of God; if any man minister, let him do it as of the ability which God giveth: that God in all things may be glorified through Jesus Christ, to whom be praise and dominion for ever and ever.
>
> (1 Peter 4:10–11)

The second section of the Ohio leaflet is on 'Christian Foundation'. This gives an account of the propitiary sacrifice and that 'no one can be saved from sin in any other way than by repentance toward God and faith in our Lord Jesus Christ' ('Welcome to our Meeting', n.d.). Jesus rose from the dead and sits at the right hand of God, where he makes intercession for humanity but at the same time 'is present among us by His Spirit to minister to us, to teach us, and to strengthen us for His service ... Christ is come to teach His people Himself'. The Holy Spirit makes Christ's 'light' available to all: 'everyone in the world has been visited by this light, and all people have God's law written in their hearts in some measure'. Given the later quotation of John 1:9, it is interesting that Christ's light is lower case: 'Only the Holy Spirit, speaking in each heart, can convince us of sin and turn us toward the forgiving love of God, which is offered to all through Jesus Christ. Only by responding in faith to Christ's light in us can we become turned from sin and made a new creation, fit to glorify and serve God' (ibid.).

The Evangelical roots of this Yearly Meeting are clear whilst the subsequent quotation from Titus on being a peculiar people harkens to a more sectarian Quakerism. In a section entitled 'Holy Scriptures', Barclay is quoted on the authority of Scripture to confirm revelation and that any revelation contrary to

Scripture is a delusion of the devil. In 'Baptism and Communion' it states that 'true baptism into Christ, and the true communion with Him, are spiritual' (ibid.). Luke 3:16 and Revelation 3:20 are quoted, but no commentary on the nature of the Last Supper is given.

Not surprisingly, given the roots of this Yearly Meeting, the emphasis is a meantime one. There is none of Fox's urgency or sense of impending endtime. Rather, its inspiration is from Barclay and an Evangelical sense of the place of Scripture and of the role of Christ. Part of the 1996 epistle from Ohio Conservative Friends read in part:

> As the Jews waited hopefully for a messiah, the carpenter's son came proclaiming the acceptable year of the Lord. To many it was blasphemous, but some believed and set about establishing the kingdom of heaven.
>
> As seventeenth century England was mired in deadly controversy over issues of church doctrine and government, the man in leather breeches [George Fox] came proclaiming that Jesus Christ had come to teach his people himself. To many it was blasphemous, but some believed and set about establishing the Society of Friends.
>
> Today, at a time when the world is in great need of spiritual healing, we again proclaim the acceptable year of the Lord, testify to our experience that Jesus Christ is come to teach us himself, and affirm his promise that when two or three are gathered in his name, Jesus Christ is present in the midst of us. To many this is still blasphemous, but some believe and know the joy God offers everyone.
>
> Come and see what our eyes have seen, hear what our ears have heard, taste what our mouths have tasted. For the Lord is good, and his mercies continue forever. Now is the time to begin anew on this beautiful morning of the Gospel Day. Begin deep down inside, where each of us stands guard over the gate of change in our hearts. Are we willing to surrender all to receive all? Then we may join together in that great stream of living water. Now it reaches out – to our families, our meetings and churches, our communities and workplaces until soon old things have passed away and behold, all things are created anew!
>
> (*Britain Yearly Meeting Proceedings*, 1997, p. 125)

This epistle doesn't sound the Day of the Lord with the same rhetorical devices as the first Friends, but certainly speaks of an intimacy with God, or of moments of intimacy. That is, following Barclay, they separated earlier understandings of living at the endtime and those of intimacy.

The North Carolina (Conservative) discipline belongs to a Yearly Meeting which was originally a schism from the Gurneyite Five Years Meeting. However, over time, it has become more influenced by Liberal Quakerism. This is because it represents the only unprogrammed Yearly Meeting in its area. Liberals moving to the area have by default joined the Meetings in this Yearly Meeting, new unprogrammed worship groups joined it for the same reason and the presence of universities in the towns of some of the Meetings has had a liberalising effect. Instead of 'Christ's light', as in the Ohio pamphlet, the Ohio and North Carolina disciplines refer to the 'Light of Christ'. However, in the Ohio one, it is the 'inward' Light; in North Carolina, 'the inner' Light (*Faith and Practice – Book of Discipline of the North Carolina Yearly Meeting (Conservative) of the Religious Society of Friends*, 1983) the phrase adopted by Rufus Jones in his North Carolina Modernist reinterpretation of Quakerism (Chapter 4). Quotations thoughout the Discipline are generally from Quaker rather than scriptural sources, although the Christian framework is clear.

On 'group worship', delineated from individual 'spiritual meditation', the discipline reads:

> The gathering of Friends in meeting for communion with God constitutes a group activity of inward prayer and contemplation. Insights gained by such spiritual activity may be spoken or left unsaid. Often they are powerful enough to move the worshipper in new directions related to the Divine plan. While the process may be called group prayer or meditation by some, Friends tend to describe it as 'waiting upon the Lord' ... The silent worship of a Quaker meeting is communion insofar as it rises above silence as a symbol and allows the life of God into the souls of the waiting group. The worshipper becomes part of the divine life, as it flows through, and transforms.
> (*Faith and Practice – Book of Discipline of the North Carolina Yearly Meeting (Conservative) of the Religious Society of Friends*, 1983, p. 15)

On the sacraments, the North Carolina (Conservative) discipline claims that the Quaker understanding differs from a normative Christian one only in that the external rituals are lacking, 'believing as we do that all life is a sacrament' (ibid., p. 16). It goes on in a less ecumenical manner, claiming that there is only one baptism, a spiritual one, and also that the true supper is set forth in Revelation 3:20. Here, as with Ohio, we can see the influence of Barclay and Gurney over Fox.

Conservative Quakerism can be seen to be about conserving the traditions of Friends. Of all the branches, they act as the most explicit reminder of some of the practices and insights of earlier generations of Friends. North Carolina (Conservative) has nine worship groups, ranging in size from a handful of members to one of seventy or so adults, with perhaps as many children.

The older Meeting Houses are still filled with Quaker benches, in most cases still facing the facing bench (sometimes raised as in Britain). In some Meetings, the benches are still divided into two halves with a middle aisle and, until recently, in at least one Meeting, men and women would sit on separate sides in worship. Some innovation has taken place in recent years with the benches forming a square or with the use of chairs (still in a square) in Meetings which meet in houses. There are generally no clocks on the walls of Meeting Houses and the Doyle Penrose picture of the Presence in the Midst hangs in an ante-room rather than the one reserved for worship. There may be some devotional literature about but it is centrally placed as in a Liberal British setting, reading in Meeting is rare. Bibles are generally absent, people bringing their own or reciting by heart as in the Quietist tradition.

Children stay in the Meeting for the whole hour or take part in a Children's Class. This is likely to be based on biblical or Quaker teaching although in more Liberal Meetings, the lives of, for example, Gandhi, or Martin Luther King might also form part of the teaching.

Ministry is less anecdotal than in Liberal settings, and usually refers to the inward relationship to God and Christ and its outward consequences. One Friend told me there was a clear understanding amongst most Conservative Friends of needing to be 'patterns and examples' in the world and thus to examine daily life carefully. Some Friends still use the plain language, a very few still wear plain dress. The Meetings are closed as led by the Elders on the facing bench by the shaking of hands, after an hour or so. The practice of other participants also shaking hands is becoming more widespread but is a recent innovation.

The Liberal Quaker Meeting

In contrast to the nine Meetings within North Carolina (Conservative), Britain Yearly Meeting contains nearly five hundred. Their settings vary but their practices are remarkably uniform, perhaps helped by the small geographical scale of the Yearly Meeting. Often chairs rather than benches are these days arranged in a circle. Raised/facing benches are generally ignored (see Chapter 6) and a table is placed centrally, usually with flowers and copies of *Quaker Faith and Practice* (1995) and the Bible. Some Meetings have flower rotas. There may be a clock in the room, perhaps a picture but the Meeting room is generally unadorned. The following is extracted from a Yearly Meeting leaflet for those attending for the first time:

> A Quaker Meeting is based on silence, but it is a silence of waiting in expectancy ... All of us are trying to come nearer to each other and to God as we are caught up in the still spirit of the Meeting ... We do not recite creeds, sing hymns or repeat set prayers. There is no ceremony, no priest, no prearranged service. Meeting for Worship starts as soon as the first person enters the room and sits down. You may find it easy to relax in the silence and thus to enter into the spirit of the Meeting, or you may be disturbed by the strangeness of the silence, by distractions outside or by your own roving thoughts. Do not worry about this, we all find it difficult to settle at times, but we return again and again to the still centre of our being, where the presence of God can be known ... The silence may be broken if someone present feels called to say something which will deepen and enrich the worship. Anyone is free to speak, pray or read aloud an appropriate passage, provided it is done in response to a prompting of the spirit which comes in the course of the Meeting. The silence is broken for the moment but it is not interrupted. Each of us brings our own life's experiences to Meeting. Some people will have a profound sense of awe and wonder because they know that God is present. Others will be far less certain. They may only be ready to hold an awareness that their experiences in life point beyond themselves to a greater whole. Some will thankfully accept God's inexhaustible love shown in Jesus, the promise of forgiveness and the setting aside of past failure. Others will know that to

seek to be open to people in a spirit of love and trust is the direction in which they want to move ...

('Your First Time in Meeting?', 1997)

This pamphlet is explanatory, balancing a theological inclusiveness with practicalities. It says what will happen and what will not, and the explanations are straightforward and not couched with reference to Quaker or scriptural authority although it does use specifically Quaker terms, such as 'speak to your condition' and 'Clerk'.

The leaflet refers to a meeting with God, but not an inward encounter with Christ. As we have seen in Chapter 4, the understanding of the outward sacraments within this tradition is one of equivalence, and optionality.

Personal accounts, collected for this book and italicised, do not help identify a specific theology of purpose or practice of worship, although spiritual concerns rank alongside those of community:

> *I also consider meeting for worship to be community formation on a profound and intimate level – and if it isn't it should be. So that is why I don't just do the coffee, and don't want to be out with the children too often. I want to see, and be part of, how this group of people explores its shared understanding and experience of the divine, and how it grows together, and apart, in the process.*

Another Friend wrote that worship was about

> *... bringing my day, my meetings before godde and bringing others and focusing on them and asking godde to be present and with them ... If I miss worship over a few days – because of time pressure, and needing to leave for work, I miss that space and often I feel as if my thoughts haven't turned to godde much recently. I do notice that something has been missing.*

Typical of a number of responses was:

> *I go to meeting for worship in order to open myself to the possibility of communion with the divine and to wait for whatever new understanding or direction may arise for me or for my meeting. I seek this communion not just for my own joy, but in a sense for the world – to play my minuscule part in the work of the Spirit. I also try to do the same in my daily life, but worshipping with others helps me to still myself and to be led to a deeper place where I am able to be more generous, more thankful and more confident in placing my gifts at the Spirit's disposal.*

Other answers were in part more personal: '*I take part fairly regularly in Meeting for Worship because I find it increasingly difficult to nurture my spiritual life on my own*', and '*Worship for me is an integral part of the rhythm of daily life. I now find I constantly attempt to "Walk, and even dance, in the Light".*'

The following was an exception in my informal survey of why people attended worship in its theological specificity: '*True worship is to obey God. Unprogrammed worship is a "Meeting for Prophesy" as described by Paul in I Corinthians 14:26–33. True worship is listening to God not talking to him or mouthing other people's words about him. It is about listening to God. About finding his will for us.*'

When asked 'What happens for you in Meeting for worship?', the answers were equally generalised in terms of theology. One Friend answered at length:

> *I send my 'aura' 'essence' 'spirit' outwards, expanding to join the general 'conscience collective'. I stay with that until someone ministers (or not). If there is ministry I use that as a focus for my energy, if it 'does not speak to my condition' i.e. I am out of synch with it. I focus on the person that was led to minister and 'send' love.*
>
> *If I cannot be 'gathered', i.e. settle down my thoughts, I read from* Faith and Practice *until I find something to link to. I always have* Faith and Practice *with me in Meeting. When I first attended Meeting, I read more. My relationship with 'God' has strengthened through this time and recently I have been able to 'pray' ...*
>
> *What happens for me is that I feel (not always) that the barriers between us and God are thinned in Meeting, that we can be attuned to each other and each other's needs and through ministry and shared silence tended. I send thanks to God for this. I feel attending Meeting brings me nearer to God and this stays with me.*

Other responses also blended the needs and joys of the human community alongside the spiritual exercise. For example:

> *Meeting provides a haven from the pressures of the World but allows one to address living there. One is an element in a palpably collected group of individuals who each bring something unique to the gathering. The early part of the meeting is almost always silent where I discipline myself to quieten racing thoughts. Usually, at some stage there is a spoken ministry and, even when it does not obviously speak to my condition, I attempt the same discipline in the following silence, searching for that element from which I can learn.*

One Friend claimed that differences in belief, or having different ways of expressing belief, was less important than the bond of community, adding:

> *For me the point of going to Meeting for Worship is to join with my community for worship ... I go to meeting because I find I am better able to 'connect' with God in the silence. The communal aspect is very important to me – I want to tell the others in the community that I feel a strong enough bond to them to worship with them.*

Another:

> *Going to meeting is exciting, because what happens is usually unexpected – the spontaneous movement of the Spirit. Quite often the communion I am waiting and*

> *hoping for does not take place. At such times I sometimes notice that others in the meeting are dozing or fidgeting or distracted. More often it seems to be me, not the meeting as a whole; times when I can't stop my mind whirring or set ego aside. But even then, the effort of attentiveness in itself feels like an offering and I nearly always gain some refreshment, if only from the pleasure of sitting with dear friends, labouring silently together.*

Community also featured in the experience of worship for this Friend: '*The most gathered part/connected part is often our ending – when we stand in a circle holding hands – and I feel the affection I have for the people I worship with.*'

For others, pleasure is less evident:

> *It varies. Rarely any kind of euphoria. The most common thing that happens is that I am able to engage in an exercise of leaving myself and all my concerns sitting on the chair in the meeting room while I rise into God's presence. That's the only way I can describe it. This presence is usually peaceful, rarely tells me anything, but leaves me changed afterwards. Once or twice I have been grabbed and held outside and beyond the meeting and led into a course of action. This did not necessarily begin in Meeting for worship, but the worship was an integral part of it.*

One Friend wrote, '*I don't usually feel "better", I may feel stretched, I may have gone to sleep.*' Another cited boredom as a hazard.

In these accounts, there is clearly an interaction with something perceived to be beyond the material, however variously described:

> *When I go to MFW I am reaching inwards and outwards towards what is beyond the Silence. This sometimes feels like reaching towards another dimension; one which is always there, but which I am not always aware of and don't always pay attention to. (For shorthand I sometimes refer to this as 'God'.) In a gathered meeting I sense that those present are doing this also; worshipping thus with others helps me become more fully present and aware of being in the Presence. There's a sense of being in love with, and loved by what's beyond the silence. Sometimes there is something I bring consciously to hold in the silence – perhaps someone who needs upholding or an issue that needs to be dealt with. I hold this in the silence, and then let go. Sometimes it feels as if, just for a moment, something crosses from beyond the silence.*

Learning was a common aspect of what people had to say about worship:

> *Sometimes I learn from the ministry of others. A particularly strong learning comes from ministry that annoys me. I analyse the source of the anger and learn much about myself. We have the habit of appointing someone to read a paragraph from* Advices and Queries. *This is often a trigger for me consulting the Christian Scriptures or* Faith and Practice *which lie on the table before us.*

One Friend referred to the more direct kind of guidance associated with the accounts of early Friends:

I have never 'heard a voice speaking to me', but am now after 61 years as a Quaker glad to become aware of anything from a 'gentle nudge' to a sense of 'presence'. The outcome is sometimes enriching, sometimes puzzling, sometimes not clearly spiritual. Sometimes – not often enough – I feel moved to actually worship – silently to praise, to give thanks, to repent ...

Another spoke of divine guidance and the place of ministry:

Sometimes not much happens in Meeting or at Meeting. I spend time thinking and trying to seek God's guidance in decisions I am having to make. Sometimes I feel like I have just made up my mind without there being any sense of divine guidance. The ministry of others is often very important and my thoughts can be led down unexpected routes by the spoken ministry of others or it can help me in my decisions – this is when I really feel that God is speaking to my condition through the words of others. I am often challenged by ministry that expresses a perspective that is different to my own. I sometimes take the opportunity to pray for/remember people I know who may be experiencing difficulties.

In terms of being prompted to give ministry, this response was typical:

Occasionally, I am moved to speak myself. I know when that happens because, unlike my experience of public speaking, I shake internally when the time comes. It is not nerves. But what it is I do not know. I try to rehearse exactly what I am going to say but when I am forced to my feet what I say is often not what I planned. Always, when I am finished, even though it may have been only a sentence or two, I feel drained. If it is near the end of meeting I have to go off on my own to recover. If a Friend ministers after me, the process of learning from his/her ministry fills me and the turmoil is stilled.

The time after Meeting was seen to be important too. Some Meetings have introduced the practice of the 'Afterword' for contributions Friends want to make which were not ministry. This can take up to half an hour. Notices may take ten minutes. After that, typically over refreshments, there is time for fellowship, for community, often lasting longer than the worship hour.

These accounts, whilst varied or enigmatic in their theology, talk much of community and even of communion. There is a shared sense of needing to leave the world and its concerns behind, to reach towards the non-material. Themes of intimacy within the Meeting and between the participant and God are clear, although often subordinate or consequential. Silence acts as the medium for an activity which incorporates an intimacy which validates the choice of method. Intimacy with God is not what prompts the liturgical form. Thus, it is not that the intimate basis of the liturgy of silence has disappeared but that its emphasis and form may be changing.

Elizabeth Collinge-Hill's work on the meaning of worship amongst four denominations concludes that despite worshipping in different ways, the specific theologies underlying the different worship forms were not explicitly mentioned by participants. Collinge-Hill concludes that the Liberal Quaker subordination of belief to experience (Dandelion, 2001, p. 178) was shared by the Roman Catholic, Methodist, and Pentecostal groups she also visited, that 'worship is serving the same purpose for people in spite of what they are supposed to believe and the forms which express them' (Collinge-Hill, 2001, p. 59). Whilst secularisation has been characterised as being about 'believing without belonging' (Davie, 1994, p. 119), Collinge-Hill claims that for those who do belong, believing is not important. The importance of community and of worshipping together was common to all the groups.

In the context of this study, what is interesting is the attitude to time and intimacy within the statements on worship made by her congregational focus groups. The Methodist statement includes no direct reference to time or intimacy but the Pentecostal one talks of communion with God: 'Worship means for us acknowledging God's greatness and majesty, surrendering to His will, and being obedient to His spirit, through communion with God and one another' (Collinge-Hill, 2001, Appendix 7).

The Roman Catholic statement was explicitly meantime looking backwards as well as forwards: 'Worship is our way of confirming our belief in God: of expressing our gratitude for all that he has done and will do for us ... ' (ibid.).

One of two Quaker groups produced the following statement:

> We see worship as based on an 'agreement to proceed' without necessarily knowing what the end will be. We have difficulty with the notion of 'worship' as veneration of an external being who requires us to offer adoration. Rather we feel as if worship is together moving into a joint spiritual space – as equals, each taking responsibility for the Meeting. In it we seek that which is of 'worth': becoming more open to ourselves and to others, experiencing at times both intense pain and joy. In worship we take the risk of exposing self, and yet often feeling a strong sense of affirmation and worth. (Ibid.)

This statement explicitly denies an external God, part of the fruits of the plausibility drive of theology in the twentieth century mentioned in Chapter 4. The risky intimacy referred to here is one of the self. The other Quaker group was explicit about intimacy: 'In our open form of worship, we can reach in the silence a loving relationship with ourselves, each other, and that which we do not yet know' (ibid.). In Chapter 7, we return to this Quaker sense of self-intimacy and how, as stated here, social intimacy may be taking over from divine intimacy. Certainly, this last statement points in that direction: self is mentioned before group, both listed before the intimacy with that not yet known, and thus, presumably, not yet fully experienced. It is this switching of the emphasis of intimacy, alongside the removal of the understanding of worship placed within a biblical understanding of time, which is central to the concluding analysis of this book.

Martin Stringer concludes his work too by claiming that there was a quest for experience (as opposed to, for example, meaning) common to the four groups he observed, although he acknowledged each group held a different focus (1999, p. 205). Ritual, for Stringer, provides a space into which experiences can be realised, claimed and articulated even in a way which renders them ultimately meaningless (ibid., p. 204). Stringer is noticing here what Gillman (see the start of Chapter 6, below), from within a faith perspective, is advocating: the extra-rational nature of religious experience and its epistemological superiority to the language often used to try and pin the experience down. The words rather are themselves symbolic, acting as a source of unity in their familiarity and ambiguity. In this sense, Stringer's analysis matches that of Liberal Christianity or liberal-Liberal Quakerism.

In contrast, the Evangelical and Conservative traditions maintain clear boundaries of permissible theology. In these traditions, theology is not symbolic or metaphorical and experience is balanced by shared meanings. In terms of the bases of liturgical practice, there are key differences between Evangelical and Conservative, and Liberal traditions already evident from Chapter 4. The Evangelical and Conservative traditions still base their explanation of worship in the foundational work of Barclay, whereas the official texts of the British Liberal Friends are not laced with the same understandings. This Barclayan understanding of worship allows the sense of operating within the biblical framework of time to remain as a foundation to the choice of liturgical form, albeit with a different sense of biblical time from the earliest Friends. Both traditions also retain a sense of intimacy with God within their idea of inward communion.

The liberal-Liberal Friends no longer justify their liturgical form in relation to Scripture or a biblical understanding of time, but, rather, in terms of the experience of the method itself. Because it works, because it isn't broken, it doesn't need fixing. In this sense, the Liberal choice of liturgical form is self-validating. Liberal Friends retain an intimacy of kinds with God (or 'God') but also one at times with the tradition and with each other. In Chapter 7, it is suggested that this diffusion of intimacy and its tendency to individualisation may lead to internal secularisation. It doesn't mean the group is any less Quaker, even if it departs from traditional understandings – although Liberals may like to be more generous towards Evangelical Friends who, outward form apart, retain a basis to worship which is very traditionally Quaker. But this analysis of liberal-Liberal Quakers may highlight the risk of the liturgical site these Friends currently inhabit.

Given this liberal-Liberal deviation from a scriptural justification of form, the following chapter looks more closely at the dynamic between speech and silence and the way in which the method of worship within this tradition is regulated in order to better understand present-day understandings of worship in that setting.

CHAPTER 6

The Means to Experience

This chapter, building extensively on Dandelion (Dandelion, P., 1996) and Collins and Dandelion (2001), combines theological and sociological readings of the silence of present-day unprogrammed liberal-Liberal Quaker meeting. (Quotations from participant observation or interview are again italicised.) Central to the use of silence and its celebration is a particular attitude to religious language. The chapter begins with this, before moving on to considering the ways speech and silence are managed within the group. The chapter concludes that the protection of the worship event through the management of silence is a means of protecting the means to experience, of primary importance within this branch of Quakerism. Experience is thus prioritised over theological understandings, the personal interpretation of experience retrospectively validating the Liberal Quaker liturgical choices. Thus, the individual has become primary in the construction and interpretation of the understanding of liturgical form.

Liberal Quakerism has become a faith of seeking. Gwyn identifies two kinds of seventeenth-century seekers which he labels as A and B types. Type A look to recover something which had been lost, the restoration of the true Church or primitive Christianity. Type B looked for a new dispensation, convinced that God would not take them backwards (Dandelion et al., 1998, p. 97). Fox managed to meld both tendencies together into a single movement. I suggest liberal-Liberal Friends represent a Type C Seeker, that is, those who prefer to seek than to find. To travel hopefully is better than to arrive, and the suggestion of a final destination point is treated with suspicion. (We will return to this below and in Chapter 7.)

Quaker writer Harvey Gillman travelled around Britain Yearly Meeting in 2002 and 2003 presenting workshops on religious language and the following is drawn from one of those events, held in Bolton in February 2003. The workshop was entitled 'Speech is impossible, silence is forbidden' and focused on the Quaker tension between feeling impelled to share and not being able to adequately.

Gillman claimed during the workshop that day that the Quaker communion of the saints is about a whole tradition of seeking rather than finding: 'Quakerism is about the Ark of the Covenant travelling through the desert, not the Temple.' In this way, the traditional Quaker opposition to creeds is reframed within a modern view of linguistic fallibility and fragility. For Gillman, the believer is in a paradoxical situation of not having the words, but, as a human, wanting to communicate. The believer simply finds the group who offers the most potential for uncovering meaning, whose storehouse of meaning may be of most help. Participants, for Gillman, are seekers after meaning.

Modern spirituality has moved away from the model of there being 'no health in us' (as from the *Book of Common Prayer* – 'Morning Prayer') to, for example, the Jonesian formulation of Light within or Matthew Fox's original blessing. Using the return to Eden as a motif, Gillman avoided explicit reference to the Second Coming whilst being able to rationalise an extreme liturgical form. Such a move towards pre-lapsarian spirituality also avoids the idea of Original Sin. Christ speaks to the disciples directly, not by means of an altar and outward sacraments and priests. For Gillman, it is pre-meantime, or even out-of-time.

No longer sharing a common theological language, it might appear as if Quakers had returned to Babel (Gen. 11:1–9), but Gillman argues that Quakers share a strong internal language, a strong peculiar language.

The key difference for Gillman, using a Wittgensteinian distinction, is between language which tells, and language which shows. The Quaker search for Eden is a search for how to live, not what to believe. Quaker theology is about showing, not telling. This echoes Janet Scott's emphasis, 'not the label but the life' (1980: 70), but also conveys something of the nature of thinking amongst present-day Quakers about theology itself, and the way theology is seen to model reality rather than accurately describe it. In this way, the meaning Quaker seekers search for is itself experiential (hence the agreement between Gillman and Stringer's work mentioned at the end of Chapter 5).

Punshon comments that theology for Liberal Friends is clearly 'empirically unverifiable' and continues to outline their view: '... statements about "God" are better approached as models rather than truths ... Since no ultimate truth can be known by definition, religion is about commitment based on open-minded enquiry, not belief' (1989, p. 27).

Gillman claims people convert to Quakerism because they've met a Quaker, that is, they've been shown in some way what a Quaker life might look like, not because they know what Quakerism is about. Indeed, given the marginalisation and individualisation of theology, the latter enquiry can be a taxing one. The danger, if there is one, is that the vocabulary of the life can sound secular. Partly, that is attractive. It diminishes differences between the speaker and the listener in a secular culture. Partly, it is risky – how are Quakers heard? Are they heard as telling?

Gillman's call to liberal-Liberal Friends is to let go of trying to possess God, but of, rather, surrendering to the vastness, to what is beyond. Gillman represents a sophisticated Quaker approach but one which is popular. It rationalises the sociological reality and the temperamental preference to say little. Below, I unpick this 'culture of silence' more systematically.

The Culture of Silence

Liberal-Liberal Friends may want to talk about their beliefs, as provisional or as partial as they are, but do not give themselves opportunities to do so. That is, the ideal of free ministry is not carried over into practice. The emphasis within the group on silence permits silent activism but also encourages it. Cultural rules around silence and speech within worship are paralleled in peripheral Quaker-time.

To speak in 'Quaker-time' outside of Meeting requires a structured opportunity to do so. Not every Meeting organises study groups or other opportunities to share belief. If discussions are arranged by a Meeting, the subject-matter may be in an area other than personal theology. In one Meeting, a series of nine study groups were all devoted to the profane. This is not unusual. Theological discussion outside of worship is impeded. The failure of the group to be thoroughly reflexive around its increased diversity is consequent upon the lack of structured opportunities to talk about belief and the lack of a safe environment in which to do so.

The 'culture of silence' is best divided into three components. First, there is the Quaker emphasis on the value of silence in theological terms. Second, the consequent devaluation of the use of speech and its appropriateness. Third, the cultural rules around ministry which operate to regulate Quaker speech acts. These components, depicted in Figure 6.1, are considered in turn.

Superficially, silence marks the boundaries of the collective worship. It is also, in Quaker orthodoxy, the medium through which God's will is heard, voiced and discerned.

It is through the silence, then, that:

- God is experienced by the individual and thus, the individual authority for belief in God is given.
- The silent approach to discerning God's will is validated through the fact that participants claim they experience God in the silence.
- God's will is discerned by the individual through 'leadings'.

Culture of Silence		
Value of Silence	Devaluation of Speech	Rules on Speech and Silence

Figure 6.1 The components of the culture of silence (Dandelion, P., 1996, p. 239)

- Ideas of what might constitute God's will are shared and tested through ministry.
- Action consequent to God's will is devised and accepted through business meeting decisions.
- The names of those playing a role in that action are thought of (in nominations committee), decided upon, and are given their authority (the appointment of Officers or committee members by the appropriate Meeting for Worship for Church Affairs).

Within the liberal-Liberal liturgy of silence, speech is devalued by consequence of the theological role given collective silence. Its status is also diminished by the popular Quaker view on a) the possibility, and b) the appropriateness, of speech to communicate belief.

First, words are not of practical use in expressing spirituality. Typical of comments recorded in interview was the response, '*All words are only blunt guesses at the truth.*' Leichty conceptualises this view in theological terms: 'God *an sich* is an utterly unknowable *X* and that what we cannot speak about, of that we must remain silent! Theology is richer and not poorer for this silence. For then we are unburdened to seek truth about the plurality of religions in the full face of the many Gods of humankind' (1990, p. 83).

Secondly, it is not appropriate to try and verbalise religious belief. This view is based on the premise that the nature of language and the nature of God are qualitatively distinct. As one Quaker commented, '*If we try* not *to be coherent, then we will be closer to God.*' Language limits the understanding of God. It can also be inappropriate: '*The lack of Quaker over-definition is one of the attractions – a fuzzy experience will lead to a fuzzy explanation; what looks exact and clear is likely to be wrong.*'

Orthodoxy mirrors the popular appeal to 'fuzzy explanation':

> Quakerism is a group of insights, attitudes, and practices which together form a way of life, rather than a dogma or creed. It rests on a conviction that by looking into their inmost hearts people can have a direct communion with their Creator. This experience cannot ultimately be described in words, but Quakers base their whole lives on it.
>
> ('The Quaker Way', 1998)

This view is not held universally: '*I feel a crucial part of any religion, including Quakerism, is a linguistic tradition, that enables people to confront themselves, their existence, moral dilemmas etc., and find wholeness and identity.*'

Opposition to a belief beyond words is a minority view, however. Hewitt neatly summates the Quaker view: 'God cannot be fitted into preformed notions bounded by expression in words. Faith must allow for elements of radical unknowability and mystery about God' (1990, p. 757). Cowie elaborates: 'Quakers, in my perception, have arrived at a novel position. The response to any direct, precise question on faith or morals has to be silence' (1990, p. 7).

In this sense, this Quaker group set themselves apart from both a text-bound tradition and an oral one:

> 'For many of us, I feel sure, putting "God" into words at all is to trivialise the very thing we are seeking to convey ... the silence of meeting means so much to me. Where else can I go to share with others what is beyond words?'
>
> (Letter to *The Friend*, 1992, **150**, p. 471)

In these ways, vocal expression of belief is devalued. By inference, the free ministry is properly concerned with that which is not beyond words. God's word, ministry, is secular in content, if sacred in origin. This position of recognising the limitations of expressing religiosity vocally is philosophically fortuitous but is undermined and contradicted by the debates around whether or not Quakers need be theists, Christians, etc. The Quaker group plays at being both rationalist, if by default, and involved in a language game of its own, at the same time.

The value placed on silence devalues speech but also increases attention on the role of vocal ministry as, necessarily, additive to that of silence (Kelly, 1944, p. 12). For all the functions of silence outlined above, ministry is the means by which those functions are expressed. If the will of God is discerned by the gathered collective, it is the vocal ministry which expresses the sense of the message.

Vocal ministry is deemed, by definition, to come from God. In the eighteenth century, Friends would minister in a nasal tone to indicate that they were only the mouthpiece of God (Chapter 3). Present-day Friends offer vocal ministry in their usual dialects and sociolects but are still confronted by two challenges. The first is to identify what is and what is not true ministry. The second is to deliver God's word in the right way. These two dimensions of establishing appropriateness are considered in turn.

The Legitimacy of Ministry

The collective experience of the group is the basis for authority of belief. Vocal ministry in this sense is 'tested' retrospectively in the subsequent silence. The challenge for the individual Friend is to attempt to determine the legitimacy (whether or not it is from God) of the message prior to its delivery:

> Each Friend who feels called upon to rise and deliver a lengthy discourse might question himself – and herself – most searchingly, as to whether the message could not be more lastingly given in the fewest possible words, or even through his or her personality alone, in entire and trustful silence. 'Cream must always rise to the surface.' True. But other substances rise to the surface besides cream; substances that may have to be skimmed off and thrown away before bodies and souls can be duly nourished. 'Is my message cream or scum?' may be an unusual and is certainly a very

homely query. Still it is one that every speaker, in a crowded gathering especially, should honestly face. Some of the dangers of silent worship can best be guarded against by its courtesies.

(Quaker Faith and Practice, 1995, 2.64)

This quotation neatly summarises the problem of discerning the legitimacy of vocal ministry. Zielinski comments, ' ... if there is any doubt in the mind of the speaker as to the value of his message, then he should remain silent' (1975, p. 31). In addition to discerning whether or not the message is from God, the Friend needs to submit to the cultural and theological rules around when and how the silence can be broken by speech if she or he is not to risk public interruption or a private word from an Elder: 'The speaker must always be sensitive to the needs and the spiritual conditions of the worshippers, remembering that through him the united exercise of the group may find a voice' (*Quaker Faith and Practice*, 1995, 2.55).

Seven aspects of normative ministry are readily identifiable. They are length, style, frequency, timing, content, thematic association and linguistic construction. These are considered in turn. The pioneering work of Davies (1988) in this area is used extensively.

Length, style and frequency are the three dimensions of vocal ministry which Elders are sanctioned to police during the Meeting for Worship. They are the public dimensions of the form of ministry. As mentioned above, participants are asked to guard against unnecessary words.

Davies found in a survey of fourteen Meetings that the length of ministry ranged between 7.5 and 20.25 minutes for the whole Meeting. Individual ministries ranged between 0.25 and 10.25 minutes. Seventy per cent of the spoken contributions were less than three minutes in duration (1988, p. 123). Ministries which are of a length greater than ten to fifteen minutes are subject to public interruption by an Elder.

It was mentioned above that Friends used to minister in a nasal tone to differentiate between their own words and those of God. Present-day Friends do not mask their own voices in the same way but participant observation revealed that a ministry sociolect existed. As the stereotype of a priest giving a sermon includes a distinct modulation, Friends subdue their voices. Displays of emotion are rare. Davies characterises vocal ministry as having a 'heavily marked style' (ibid., p. 133).

For what are probably secular, not theological, reasons the orthodox advice is to minister no more than once in Meeting for Worship. In a disrupted Meeting containing eleven ministries, four from one person, it was the multiple nature of the contributions, rather than their length or style, which allowed an Elder to intervene.

Timing is important too: 'Wait to be sure of the right moment for giving the message ... Beware of making additions towards the end of a meeting when it was well left before' (*Quaker Faith and Practice*, 1995, 2.55). There are 'right moments' for speech. Discerning the right moment is about both obedience to God's will, and awareness of the time-frame of worship. The acknowledgement of the tension between the two is sometimes made explicit, as in the following quotation: '*I know it is virtually closing time but I did want to say* ...'.

There are also 'right moments' for other sorts of noise. The following pattern of silences was recorded at one Meeting:

> *The people came in in stages. Whilst the door was still open, people were silent but smiling at each other, greeting each other silently. Gradually, they adopted 'worship positions' which were held whilst latecomers were let in a few minutes later. At each ministry, there was a general shuffle, coughs, and the blowing of a nose. The exception was a very faint ministry when this process of readjustment took place immediately after the end of ministry. After forty-five minutes, the children came in. Friends lifted their heads, opened their eyes, smiled at the children, before the final period of silence.* (Field Notes)

One movement is a signal for many. Noise levels rise when accompanying breaks in the liturgical ritual of silence occur: when one person breaks the silence, to minister, leave, or enter, others take the opportunity to make themselves comfortable for the subsequent return to silence.

Davies talks of 'non-mentionables' or those subjects which 'are just not among the mentionables'. He cites insults, contributions which require an answer (such as the making of arrangements), and items which have no relevance or significance to the group (1988, p. 131). Non-mentionables are of at least three sorts. First, there are those which are inappropriate to the exercise. Davies' examples are of this sort. *Quaker Faith and Practice* reminds Friends: 'Ask wisdom of God that you may be sure of your guidance and be enabled humbly to discern and impart something of his glory and truth' (*Quaker Faith and Practice*, 1995, 2.55).

If the British Quaker 'God' is constructed as essentially loving and benign (Dandelion, P., 1996, p. 161), then ministry will need to reflect this, if it is to fit in with the group culture. Similarly, and secondly, ministries which deny the idea that there is 'that of God in everyone', one of the few beliefs held almost universally within liberal-Liberal Quakerism, are likely to be countered, by a reactive ministry or, more gently, by an additional contribution later in the Meeting:

> *When a Friend spoke of his dislike of 'the dangerous fundamentalism' of Catholics and Muslims, one newcomer rose immediately following the contribution to counter the message. Another Friend rose towards the end of the Meeting to offer a message of love and acceptance. I assumed this message was directed at both the previous speakers.* (Field Notes)

Thus, religious sensibilities determine the limits of freedom of the minister.

The third type of unmentionable is that which might offend the secular sensibilities of other participants. For example, subjects such as abortion or contraception are rarely, if ever, mentioned in ministry.

Hubbard has noted how 'the sequence of contributions to a Meeting develops, usually in a fairly logical and associative manner, from one speaker to another'

(1992, p. 198). Similarly, Davies has noted that whilst the content of ministry can vary, '[t]he tendency is to restrict the coverage on any one Meeting for Worship occasion' (1988, p. 128): 'There is topic placement in ministry chains. In particular, there is a seizure of the first topic as a lead into subsequent contributions' (ibid., p. 129).

The normative pattern of ministry is for a series of thematic ministries to add to the opening contribution. This archetype does not mean that distinctive variations do not occur. However, as Flanagan states, of those involved in liturgical performances, 'actors learn to recognise what is undesirable' (1991, p. 165). In this way, standard practice transforms habit into orthodoxy and transmits it as such.

Davies concludes his valuable work on the Meeting for Worship as a language-learning event with the observation that Meeting for Worship is both a social occasion and a speech event: 'As in other speech events such as single conversations, there are forward and back references (e.g. "last week in Meeting") but to members, a Meeting for Worship is also a social occasion in which ministry is normal and in which items of ministry inter-relate' (1988, p. 133).

Mention has already been made of normative length of contribution, delivery style, acceptable content, and the likelihood of thematic association with other ministries. In addition to these dimensions of the construction of the ministry performance, there is a linguistic association with other ministries within any one Meeting in terms of the words used. Davies, in his study of Quaker ministry as a language-learning process, showed how a considerable cohesion of language cut across different speakers. Key words enter into successive ministries (ibid., p. 129). As with the thematic association of ministry, this association of words can be analysed in terms of the operation of the 'accommodation model': 'an individual can induce another to evaluate him more favourably by reducing dissimilarities between them' (Giles and Powesland, 1975, p. 157).

The existence of rules around the seven aspects, described above as part of the behavioural creed, does not necessarily undermine the potential of all ministry to come from God. Rosenberg's work on spontaneous sermons demonstrates how the sermons he studied followed certain rules of construction and metre whilst maintaining a spontaneity of content (1970). The rules operate to safeguard the perceived validity of vocal ministry and to maintain worship in a normative form: 'the autonomous defining qualities of this form of ritual have to be serviced and kept secure in a tactful manner so that tacit assumptions can be protected. These are deemed to be vulnerable and are associated, crucially, with the intended definition of the situation' (Flanagan, 1991, p. 153).

There are four consequences to the rules around speech and silence in worship. The first is that silence is an active entity and that the correct use of silence and speech is a skill to be learned. Second then, conversely, silence can be misused or ignored resulting in the abuse of the operation of the free ministry. Third, fear of not having learnt the normative style of, or misusing, speech acts as self-censor within worship. Fourth, fear of conflict and ostracism impedes 'talking-God' outside of the worship event. These four consequences are considered in turn.

The phrase of Barclay that it is impossible to counterfeit silence (Barclay, 2002, p. 311) is oft-quoted. Theological meaning aside, it pinpoints the need for the individual Quaker to learn about the use of silence in a Quaker context. At an empirical level, it is incorrect. As Flanagan states: 'The uncheckable nature of rite could allow piety to be feigned, devoutness to be parodied, and deceits to prosper by an actor with sufficient wit to keep a holy face ... He could be the deceiving beneficiary of what cannot be checked' (1991, p. 115). Within Quakerism, the holy face can take different forms. People sit in different ways, some with their palms upturned, others with their hands folded. The following quotation from a Friend in New Zealand interestingly links the decision to close or keep eyes open during worship with a specific theological understanding of the process of worship: 'I am an open-eyed Friend ... I do like to see the people I'm worshipping with. (Don't take readily to the Via Negativa.)' (Child, 1995, p. 13).

Friends engage in all sorts of activities during worship (see Figure 7.1 in Chapter 7). One Meeting held a special discussion on how to avoid falling asleep in Meeting. Friends acknowledged a plethora of sophisticated methods for centring down. Others talked about how they often felt their distracted minds interfere with the silence for others, that is, that it would decrease the unity and power of the approach to God. In a questionnaire administered in 1989, 22.2 per cent found their initial major reaction to silent worship was concern with the problem of daily thoughts interfering (Dandelion, P., 1996, p. 251). Figure 7.1 illustrates that 65.7 per cent of respondents claimed that 'thinking' best described what they did in Meeting for Worship: 'The silence with its unboxed edges, freedom and depth, provides a safe space to think the unthinkable, explore the unformed and simply to be' (Letter to *The Friend*, 1990, **148**, p. 1520).

Experienced Friends emphasised their ability to discern the real event from the counterfeit: '*It's a verbal silence but is not just silence, more like a calm awareness – you can sense when a Meeting is gathered.*' Samarin has called the meaningful use of silence the 'language of silence' (1965, p. 115). It is this language which newcomers to the group learn how to use for both silent and vocal ministry.

Paradoxically, these cultural rules are learnt *in situ*: 45 per cent of the survey respondents claimed that they first began to learn about what Quakers believe 'by watching and listening to others'; 37.4 per cent cited vocal ministry as a learning medium (Dandelion, P., 1996, p. 251): '*The jargon in notices is very muddling – I would have liked a general explanation. Most of what I have learnt has come through the ministry.*'

The emphasis on quiet at Meeting for Worship and cogency at Meetings for Worship for Church Affairs, coupled with the complexity of the routine, encourages newcomers to keep quiet. Even if they are confident, sensitivity that the routine is important often entails only a gradual vocal involvement with business matters: '*I sat and watched for about six months before I felt able to contribute at Preparative Meeting. The process took even longer at Monthly Meeting but that was because I did not go every time.'*

Where the behavioural rules are largely hidden and learnt through sitting in the silence itself, a busy meeting offers a 'Catch 22' situation in terms of normative socialisation in Quaker culture. The ministry may offer guidelines for belief but may also detract from the teaching of a collective behavioural norm. Friends are always requested to attend Quaker funerals and weddings where large numbers of non-Friends will be attending in order to strengthen the orthodoxy of worship.

The newcomer is at least afforded the possibility of sitting still and doing nothing, although many still worry about procedure: '*The person next to me stood up and spoke about five minutes into the Meeting. I wondered if I was supposed to go next.*' As Heilman notes, spiritual states are not easy to perceive: 'The adroit shul Jew knows well how to be immersed in prayer while in reality leaving his mind elsewhere' (1976, p. 140).

In the same sense that it is possible to counterfeit silence, it is possible to counterfeit ministry. *Quaker Faith and Practice* warns explicitly: 'Pray that your ministry may rise from the place of deep experience, and that you may be restrained from unnecessary and superficial words' (1995, 2.55). The Quaker tradition, to operate without a differentiated priesthood, rests on claims that ministry is legitimate in form as well as content (Bauman, 1983, p. 35).

The predictability of timing and content of ministry increases the cynicism of some Friends as it impresses others:

> Spoken ministry can be irrelevant to many, sometimes trivial, often repetitive because of the tendency of the same members to minister, and occasionally quite inappropriate, so often beginning in music hall fashion – 'As I was on my way to Meeting this morning', or offensive ... the freedom to minister will sometimes lead to abuse ...
>
> (Davies, 1988, p. 109)

Zielinski counters the idea of the blame for flawed ministry resting with the individual. He claims there is no need to 'control or evaluate the content of a message' if it arises out of a gathered Meeting (1975, p. 30). Individual discernment is replaced by collective devotion as the check on the legitimacy of 'God's word'. The requirement of individual discipline of discernment is replaced by the discipline of the individual commitment to the group devotion. Again, orthodoxy portrays silence as more than just the collection of the absence of individual noise.

Popular views about those who misuse ministry are not congruent with Zielinski's idealism. In response to how Friends would react to hearing sermons as a regular part of their religious life, many respondents quipped that they already did, in Meeting for Worship.

The idea of individual wrong (either through misuse or ignorance of the rules) is reinforced by the occasional intervention by Elders mid-ministry when an individual has spoken for too long. Although instances of eldering are not common, the acts are mythologised through gossip and storytelling. Sensationalism of this sort operates as a control mechanism in itself (cf. Weick, 1987): *'I heard far more tales of people being asked to end their ministry than I did of welcome ministry. I remember a momentary pause just before I first ministered and the dread thought rushed into my head that I would be asked to sit down.'*

One *'self-confessed cynic'* believed individual reticence was more widespread than the group would believe, and claimed: *'If Quakers voted, 22 per cent would carry the minute. The other 78 per cent are shy, fed up, or not listened to.'* Non-involvement can masquerade as piety in a group where sitting in silence is so highly valued.

Of the questionnaire sample, 52.2 per cent of non-Members, and 55.3 per cent of those affiliated with the group less than three years, had never ministered. Only around one in five group members ministered within a year of their regular participation. Nearly a quarter of the sample had never ministered (Dandelion, P., 1996, p. 254).

There is a parallel between this reticence and a) the learning curve, and b) the fear of getting it wrong. Heron found 15 per cent of 'Attenders' (those who attend regularly but who are not in formal membership) felt that other Attenders might not formally join because they did not feel 'good enough' (1992, p. 27). Whilst Heron's response item refers to a broader frame of reference than knowledge of procedure, embarrassment acts as a continual threat to participation, and a connection might be found between fear of inadequacy and the rules surrounding silence and speech. The recording of ministers was abolished in 1924 in the belief that the practice hindered the free ministry.

The free ministry is not utilised by all and is more likely to be used by those with a longer affiliation with the group. Self-confidence plays a large part in being prepared to act as a channel for God's word. For some, there is no choice:

> ... as the minutes ticked by and I sat in the healing peace I began to be aware that something inside me was formulating a question which urgently needed to be asked ... My heart was pounding uncomfortably and I began to shiver ... To start with I resisted this prompting. I looked around the room and noticed several Friends before whom I was reluctant to make a fool of myself. I could not get up and speak in front of them. I would rather die first. The shaking and pounding diminished a little ... But not for long ... This time I told myself 'I'll count twenty and then if no one else has spoken I shall have to' ... I counted twenty and then fifty and still no one spoke. Now I sat conscious only of this overpowering force which was pushing me to my feet until finally I had to give in to it.
>
> (*Quaker Faith and Practice*, 1995, 2.58)

For many, ministry is an act consciously decided on in which human predisposition might *'wrestle with divine will'*.

Rules are about the protection of the means to experience. Experience is crucial for Friends, central in the Liberal project in terms of authority and insight, and thus the means to it is policed (by, for example, Clerks and Elders who manage the silence) and protected. Gerald Hughes writes of a similarly orthodox interpretation of the right way to celebrate Mass. Seminary students who had danced at the end of Mass in celebration were subsequently forbidden to celebrate Mass in that way: 'We had to go to the chapel, which was cold and uncomfortable, where they sat shivering in serried ranks while something died in them. All this was done in the name of "reverence, otherwise you don't know where it will end" ' (Hughes, 1986, p. 36).

When some Quakers celebrated the end of the Summer Gathering in Lancaster in 1995 with drumming and footstomping, one correspondent to *The Friend* claimed this activity was tempting the wrath of God (Letter to *The Friend*, 1995, **153**, p. 1182). As Martin suggests, there is a problem with the sensuality and emotionalism of the over-expressive: 'there has, therefore, been a tendency, persistent though not at all universal, for the religious "register" to be regarded as slow and square rather than curvy or bouncing. God is to be praised slowly' (2002, p. 53).

The other axis of expression to be negotiated within the group, as suggested in Chapter 3, is the degree to which the religious aesthetic precludes or shrouds the worldly. Binns emphasises the mystery of worship in his description of Orthodox liturgy:

> The visitor is confronted by a mysterious and many-sided activity ... He [*sic*] finds that the worship is sung to an unfamiliar and haunting beauty ... the altar cannot be seen as it is concealed behind a solid wooden screen covered in icons arranged in rows (iconostasis), or perhaps a curtain ... The walls are also covered with paintings, called frescoes. The sense of mystery and awe is increased by the dimly lit interior, glittering with candles, or oil lamps, or perhaps, less aesthetically, coloured electric light bulbs ... it is a meeting of God and humanity.
>
> (2002, pp. 39–40)

Those who have campaigned for the retention of the centrality of the Book of Common Prayer have emphasised the importance of the mystery of worship (Homan, 2001):

> Nothing could be more unlike the scene of the Last Supper than a High Mass according to the Roman rite. And yet any other method than the one employed by the Church would have resulted, as it often has among Protestants, in little more than the reproduction of the outward order in which, for a moment of time, God willed to give the freest and fullest expression of Himself. It may be that much of our modern painting and literature has, in its pursuit of realism, been betrayed by the same purpose – seeking to express what lies behind the actual phenomena by a slavish imitation of the facts that conceal it.
>
> (Walke, 2002, p. 160)

Otto claimed: 'No form of devotion which does not offer or achieve this mystery for the worshipper can be perfect or can give lasting contentment to a religious mind' (1923, p. 219).

Mystery and the sense of possibility it engenders is crucial for Friends too. As Crumbine suggests, 'Silence is the revelation of concealment, the "saying" of mystery' (1975, p. 148). Liberal Quakers on holiday away from Quaker Meeting are most likely to prefer a high-church service to a low one, prioritising mystery over literalness even at the expense of simplicity. Freiday has noted that Friends have linked inward communion with the elevation of the host in the Mass (1967, p. 241).

Quakers claim of course that they can worship anywhere, although one group I taught claimed it was impossible to worship in a chapel they described as gaudy. Both Collins (1996, and Coleman and Collins, 2000) and Homan (2000) have detailed the present-day Quaker aesthetic.

There is a distinct Quaker aesthetic and fashion to the unprogrammed Meeting House. In Britain, the central table with flowers and the book of discipline, perhaps a Bible, has become standard. Flower rotas ensure what Collins has called the 'not-altar' meets the expectations of familiarity. Coming from elsewhere, overseas Friends have commented that the prominence of this arrangement struck them as resembling an altar:

> Even the unprogrammed Friends meeting for worship has a ritual quality to it, that much is clear. The elements of the rite may not include Eucharist, prayers of confession, or benediction, but the gathering together, the centering, the silence, the handshake, are all 'customary forms' which amount to a reasonably structured environment creating space for the visitation of Presence and for the communal management of Absence.
>
> (Johns, 1998, p. 34)

Peter Collins has devised the term 'plaining' to refer to the social construction of an aesthetic impulse within Quaker space, symbolisng a theological and counter-cultural impulse (1996). In their work on a Quaker habitus (see Chapter 3), Coleman and Collins cite 'the plain' as 'a constant meta-narrative which informs much of contemporary Quaker faith and practice' (Coleman and Collins, 2000, p. 325). The Meeting House is a particularly focused area for the expression of habitus (ibid.). It is no longer a symbol of 'anywhere' or of 'all places' but has become the conveyer of deeper social and theological meaning, a site of theological and sociological transmission. The internal architecture mirrors a religious and political levelling, 'the plain' affirming and encouraging a particular aesthetic set of choices found throughout this branch of Quakerism. Quaker property has become its own form of outreach and inreach. Picturesque seventeenth-century Meeting Houses attract tourists as well as acting as historical sites to nurture the faith. At places like Brigflatts near Sedbergh in Cumbria, the plain interior is rich with theological intention of a complex simplicity. The beauty of the location, hills rising up in front of the Meeting House conveys to some of the Quakers who visit a physical continuation between built environment and this rural part of 'God's backyard'. The past has replaced the future as a focus for Quakers seeking inspiration.

Messenger claims that even radical Protestants never fully managed to avoid visible representation of the sacred (1999, p. 51). He connects the layout of the revival camp with the spiritual processes of conversion and perfection with radial streets between the tents leading to the centre of revival energy and action. Physical movement towards the middle mirrored spiritual process towards conversion (ibid., p. 58; see also Weiss, 1987, p. 120) Perfection, on the other hand, Messenger comments, involved a different process. Some, he claims, could cite a specific moment of sanctification, but for others it was an outward state that reflected an inward reality already achieved. Ordered living within a system of mutual accountability, accommodated and encouraged by the intimacy and openness of tent living, tents only inches apart, reflected the inward state of grace (Messenger, 1999, p. 58):

> The architecture of holiness represented the mythic pilgrimage dwellings of God's people while also displaying a picture of perfect citizens in the perfect city to come ... the tents, cottages, hotels, roominghouses, auditoriums, and landscape were instrumental in creating specific performances of conversion/holiness. At frontier meetings, tents ringed the campground clearing, forming the threshold of sacred space. This circle of tents contained and focused religious activity like a large parabolic dish, driving the emotional energy backs towards the center of the arena. Only by crossing outside this circle of tents could one escape the pressing calls for total involvement in ritual performance.
>
> (ibid., p. 53)

In the Quaker context, those who manage the space often define it. Doorkeepers may slow down those rushing in late through their control of the door, thus protecting the silence within. The arrangement of the furniture may also provide tensions between theological interpretations and personal preferences. Since the abolition of the recorded ministry in 1924, the raised 'facing benches' once inhabited by recorded Ministers have often fallen into disuse. Chairs may be placed in front of the bench or the room rearranged to marginalise the bench. I heard one report of wardens marking it off-limits through simply not dusting that area. In another Meeting House, the cups and saucers for after-Meeting refreshments were stacked there. Sometimes these choices are made more visible by negotiation of the actors at the start of Meeting. In one Meeting, cushions were removed from the facing bench and distributed onto nearby chairs. When one Friend took a cushion off a chair and moved to the facing bench, she was asked to sit somewhere else. In another Meeting, an Elder rose to restart a ticking clock ten minutes into worship. In a Meeting divided over the use of a central table, one Elder rearranged the furniture in order to move the table into the centre five minutes after the worship had officially begun. The protection of the means to experience often manifests itself in particularly outward ways.

Peter Collins and I have used the work of Joy Hendry to try and theorise the social control of spontaneity within the Quaker setting (Collins and Dandelion, 2001). In her work (1993) on Japanese culture, Hendry developed the theory of wrapping as a cultural template or cultural design for life in Japan. She found in her research that the physical wrapping of gifts, often many times, and typically perceived to be of greater cultural importance than the gift itself, was part of a whole range of wrapping practices within Japanese life. The Japanese wrap gifts with considerable care and attention to the most minute details using a diverse range of materials – paper, straw, cloth, wood and so forth. She further found that wrapping extends from the material into the linguistic. Hendry describes how 'respect' language (*keigo*) was an agent of wrapping, that bodies and space were as numerously and as literally wrapped as gifts, and that in other ways, ritual and political life were wrapped.

Hendry remarks, 'wrapping ... separates (the gift) from the dirt and pollution of the outside world' (ibid., p. 23). The wrapping of ritual practice is a critically important endeavour in the context of religious faith and practice. Apart from constituting a boundary (or intricate series of boundaries), it also marks off two groups, 'us' and 'them', one from the other; the former clean and Godly, the latter defiled and un-Godly. There is, however, a price to pay for this differentiation. The cost is the difficult task faced by participants, especially newcomers, who need to assimilate often subtle and ambiguous wrapping practices. And it is important that they do – in order to identify fully with the group, to participate 'properly' in worship and in order to avoid unwittingly blurring the boundary between 'us' and 'them'.

Again, as Hendry remarks in relation to Japanese gifts, 'There is certainly a notion of power associated with an enclosed state, like that of a child in the womb, in Japanese folklore, which includes stories about supernatural children born from a peach, a gourd, and a segment of bamboo' (ibid., p. 25). It is possible, then, that the 'wrapped' group derives a sense of power, of authority, whether divine or secular, from its layers of wrapping. Religious groups attempt to limit the easy dispersal of arcane knowledge and practice and one means of ensuring this is through a restricted use of language itself: ' ... the power which an ability to use certain forms of language may hold, particularly where this ability is restricted to closed groups of people. This power is derived partly from the status ascribed to the linguistic wrapping involved' (ibid., p. 67).

In Japan, Hendry found that the practices involved with an approach to the sacred were the least wrapped (ibid., p. 61). Sacred offerings are left out unwrapped and when people talk to the deities they drop the polite (wrapped) language. As she says, 'Like the offerings they make, they present themselves entirely unwrapped, free from any of the social packaging with which they need to confront other human beings' (ibid., 62). However, Peter Collins and I suggest that worship among nonconformist religious groups which are characterised by immediate and unmediated religious experience, demonstrates surprisingly well-developed and effective modes of wrapping. The most interesting and significant thing about these wrapping practices is the ways in which they simultaneously conceal and reveal religious spontaneity, structuring and channelling the reception, celebration and communication of the Word (Collins and Dandelion, 2001).

As with food packaging, the wrapping protects (Hendry, 1993, p. 18). From the inside, the wrapping protects the reliability of the events and an anarchism possible within the concept of the free ministry. Wrapping and its inherent controlling function also constrains direct unmediated access by layering rules onto the practise of universal ministry. In this way, wrapping adds a layer or surprise, in the manner of a present (ibid., p. 13). It also introduces an element of ritual, adding to the power of the liturgy. Hendry explains that wrapping works 'to refine the object, to add to it layers of meaning which it could not carry in its unwrapped form' (ibid., p. 27).

Quaker worship is not merely silence: there are the four consequences to the rules around speech and silence in worship mentioned above. The first is that silence is an active entity and that the correct use of silence and speech is a skill to be learned. The second is that the skill can be misused or ignored resulting in the abuse of the operation of the free ministry. Third, fear of not having learnt the normative style of, or misusing, speech acts as self-censor within worship. In other words, the management of the unmediated constrains entry into the means of accessing and expressing the sacred. Newcomers have to learn the rules and language in which the sacred is wrapped or risk their path to assimilation in the sectarian ranks. Combined with the value placed on silence, the strictures on speech within silent worship viewed from the outside undermine the concept of the free ministry and foster a normative silence rooted in fear rather than obedience. They legitimate the status quo and lend power to those vested with the maintenance and interpretation of the rules. In this way, the sect limits the progress of participants in gaining expertise, and thereby limits the ability of any one individual to influence the group.

Elders, whilst not separated outwardly are 'socially wrapped' within the group, obscured from view, hidden. As the rules of silence need to be learnt, so do the roles of those masked within the circle of worshippers. At the same time, two Elders may sit in the centre of Meeting so that their closing handshake is public and visible. As in the schools and offices of Japan (Hendry, 1993, p. 124), the Elders sit wrapped by the benches and by those who sit upon them, at the heart of the Meeting. This could signify their closer proximity to the corporate communication with the divine but it also signals their central role in the control of constraint. Their handshake ends the temporal wrapping of silence and the people gathered in worship return to a normative style of interaction and conversation.

The wrapping is sometimes negotiated, especially where leadership is diffuse or absent. Where no one is appointed to end the Meeting, the silence can carry on beyond the formal time 'marked' for it. Equally, if the length of worship is unspecified, as happened at one young Friends' gathering, it may end more than once with a diminishing group of worshippers ignoring attempts to end the silence. The example of the Meeting divided over the location of the table is another example of the wrapping of worship being negotiated between participants.

In the 1970s, the shaking of hands at the end of worship was extended by popular innovation to the whole of the Meeting whereas before only Elders had performed this ritual. (Some believe such innovation was imported from the Anglican church where sharing the peace was being expressed in a similarly inclusive way.) Until very recently, at least some Friends refused to participate in this democratised ending, one persistently claiming 'I'm not a shake-hand Friend!'

Whilst Quaker theology involves an unwrapping of the worshippers as they seek to go deeper into the silence (cf. Hendry, 1993, p. 151), the wrapping of the sacred in silence, and the wrapping of the means of access to the sacred, ensures conformity. The degree to which the 'behavioural creed' (see Chapter 4 above) is maintained encourages a conservatism within the group.

If choices over early Quaker worship embodied and reflected an experience, modern Quaker worship safeguards the means to experience. From the choice of liturgical form as consequence, it has become a means to an end, a definitional characteristic of 'unprogrammed' Quakerism, or even an end in itself.

The previous sections of this chapter have considered the constraints placed on speaking in worship through the value placed on silence over speech, the rules surrounding the transmission of God's word, and the fear of diminishing that value or breaking the rules. It is argued that these aspects of normative Quaker culture foster a culture of silence outside of worship too. Keeping quiet involves less risk than sharing belief.

Through the invisibility of belief, fostered by the culture of silence, change in individual and group belief is both accommodated and concealed: 'There are those who will say that our unity lies in the silence of our meetings for worship, a silence beyond words and ideas. That silence can also be used as a cloak to cover up and smother our disunity, in which nothing considered "divisive" can be uttered or done' (Letter to *The Friend*, 1992, **150**, p. 604). The lack of a vocal confession of faith, or a structural requirement to subscribe to any set of words, allows silence over matters of belief to continue. This silence is supported by a fear of self-induced ostracism. Where Friends do speak out, it is as individuals who, within the concept of continuing revelation, may change their view. The larger-scale picture of theological allegiances remains obscured.

In the past, the invisibility of belief would not have been problematic: Friends had a greater unity over matters of belief and could assume knowledge of each other's theology; there was less fear of isolation, due to the wider use of religious language. Present-day British Quakerism is confronted with a theological diversity which remains unchecked and uncheckable and unknown. Figure 6.2 illustrates the operation of the culture of silence.

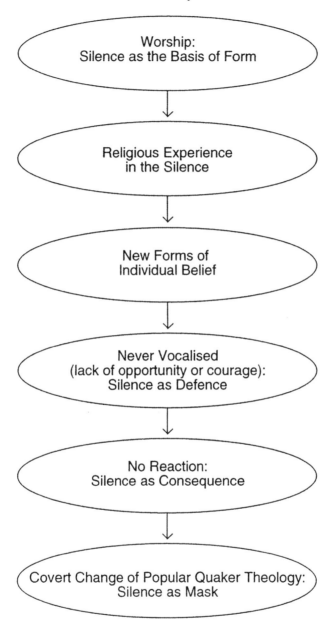

Figure 6.2 The operation of the culture of silence (Dandelion, P., 1996, p. 258)

At the top of Figure 6.2 is worship and the use of silence as the basis of Quaker form. Quaker religious experience occurs within the silence, and types of individual belief are constructed to help make sense of that experience. Belief may be vocalised in ministry but frequently is not, either through a lack of opportunity or lack of courage (with the silence used as a form of self-censor or defence against ostracism). The lack of vocalisation of belief means that there is no reaction. The silence operates at this stage of the process as a consequence of a) silence used as a form of worship, and b) silence used as a defence. In this way, changes to popular belief, as newcomers enter the group or as participants change the language of the theology, occur covertly. This process can repeat itself continually. Changes in individual and group belief remain hidden (silence masks reality) whilst the common form of worship presents a picture of unity.

Thus, the silence operated by liberal-Liberal Friends can conceal diversity, both of theology, and of the theology of worship. Whilst the form of worship operates as a means of cohesion to the group, its varying interpretations may at some stage begin to unpick the form. The meeting for worship for business, for example, also based in silence has been traditionally seen as a means to the discernment of the will of God. For those without a God or a God with a will, this formula becomes anachronistic. Instead, for these Friends, the business method becomes a temperamental or political preference. What was once a heretical query, 'why can't we vote?', becomes a legitimate question.

The form still creates a boundary to Quakerism but it is one whose popular understanding is in transition. The policing and wrapping of form in the ways described above protect the means to experience and contain the expression of experience respectively. These social mechanisms do not protect or contain theological understandings of worship. Those theological understandings are as equally individuated as any aspect of the liberal-Liberal theological enterprise. Liberal-Liberal theology as a specific collective category increasingly does not exist and that shift from earlier Quakerism has inherently incorporated a move away from a scriptural understanding of basis of unprogrammed worship and could incorporate the demise of a sense of collective intimacy with God.

CHAPTER 7

Reading Liberal Silence: New Intimacies and the End of Time

> The excellency of this silent waiting upon God doth appear in that it is impossible for the enemy, viz. The devil, to counterfeit it.
>
> (Barclay, 2002, p. 311)

This chapter concludes the book by trying to explore the differences between the worship of the first Friends and their liberal-Liberal descendants, and by asking how far a faithful life can be sustained without any outward reminders, particularly when the inward experience may be diffuse or privatised. In other words, what happens to a form of liturgy when the bases upon which it was constructed (in our reading here, a sense of the endtime, and an explicit and continuous intimacy with God) may have fallen away? Contrary to Barclay's quotation above, this chapter suggests that there is a danger for liberal-Liberal Friends of silence no longer bringing presence into absence, but being in and of itself only silence.

We need to be careful, of course, of overplaying the seventeenth-century context. It may be that George Fox and a few other leaders had a particularly acute experience of the divine simply not shared by most Quakers. It may be that most Quakers did not hold a sense of unfolding endtime or feel wrapped in a continuous intimacy with God. Perhaps it was the preaching of these Friends who had been given a fuller measure of the light that inspired the movement and acted as a means to faithfulness in the last days of meantime. Perhaps Friends needed to worship together because of the very lack of shared experience. Otto responds to the idea that asking for the 'presence of the divine' may be redundant given God's omnipresence:

> Such a view is often put forward, and with a confident air of assurance which is in sharp conflict with the testimony of genuine religious experience; so much so, indeed, that one is tempted to venture a very blunt reply to it. We say, then, that this doctrine of the omnipresence of God – as though by a necessity of His being He must be bound to every time and every place, like a natural force pervading space – is a frigid invention of metaphysical speculation, entirely without religious import. Scripture knows nothing of it. Scripture knows no 'Omnipresence', neither the expression nor the meaning it expresses; it knows only the God who is where He wills to be, and who is not where He wills not to be, the 'deus mobilia', who is no mere universally extended being, but an august mystery, that comes and goes, approaches and withdraws, has its time and hour, and may be far or near in infinite degrees, 'closer than breathing' to us or miles remote from us. The hours of His 'visitation' and His 'return' are rare and solemn occasions, different essentially not only from the 'profane' life of every day, but also from the calm confiding mood of the believer,

whose trust is to live ever before the face of God. They are the topmost summits in the life of the Spirit. They are not only rare occasions, they must needs be so for our sakes, for no creature can bear often or for long the full nearness of God's majesty in its beatitude and its awfulness. Yet there must still be such times, for they show the bright vision and completion of our sonship, they are bliss in themselves and potent for redemption. They are the real sacrament, in comparison with which all high official ceremonials, masses, and rituals the world over become the figurings of a child. And a Divine Service would be the truest which led up to such a mystery and the riches of grace which ensue upon the realization of it.

(1923, pp. 219–20)

Otto thus both supports a Quaker theology of liturgy whilst denying the possibility of the early Friends' claim that they were in a constant state of intimacy. Certainly there are clues in early Quaker writing that suggest a 'deus mobilia'. Pennington's pre-Quaker convincement experience left him praying for a reduction in grace as it was too much to bear (see Chapter 1), mirroring Otto's comment here about how the sense of presence needs to be fleeting given its awfulness.

Howgill's mention of God appearing daily to him and his friends (see Chapter 1) implies a disappearing too; the theology behind holding worship at any time and in any place is not about a constancy of sacramentality as much as a constant potential for it.

David Johns cites Chauvet's sense of paradox about liturgy: 'The assembly of Christians gathered in the name of Christ or his memory is ... the first sacramental representation of presence. At the same time, it is the first stumbling block for faith, for such a representation is also the radical mark of absence' (Chauvet, 1995, p. 187). In other words Chauvet sees the gathering signifying both presence and absence: 'it is not self-evident that it is he, the living Lord, who presides over the assembly' (ibid.). Johns adds: 'Silence may lead nowhere else than to the terrifying realization that there is no thing there; silence may be our awkward assertion that God does not exist' (1998, p. 32). For Quakers who have a constant sense of accompaniment, this potential for absence is simply not there – gathering doesn't signify absence, merely intentional collectivity. One Friend described Meeting for Worship as intentional sacramentality (as opposed to the incidental sacramentality of the rest of life).

This perpetual sacramental possibility undermines the idea of claiming special virtue for one day of the week. In terms of an understanding of what can be achieved outside 'all high official ceremonials, masses, and rituals', Otto and early Friends are in accord.

The question we need to face here is the extent to which liberal-Liberal Friends still maintain even a glimpse of heaven as part of their liturgical practice. If we accept the idea that liturgy is a means to help the people of God remain faithful in the meantime, then given the absence of any means to remembrance, what keeps Liberal Friends faithful or rather, and/or to what are they faithful?

For Messenger, in his study of Ocean Grove, the maintenance of its religious identity depends on the remembrance of its holy days and holy times (1999, p. 131).

The move from the prescription of rest on Sunday with the ban on driving to the suggestion of rest symbolises a permissiveness and diffusion of identity that undermines the holy.

Liberal-Liberal Friends do not remember through a sense of outward time. Carrdus (1993) has charted the growth of the celebration of Christmas amongst British Friends, but it is not corporately celebrated as an outward remembrance, a means of keeping the faith. Rather, whilst the testimony to times and seasons is incorporated in the latest British Quaker book of discipline (*Quaker Faith and Practice*, 1995, 27.42) it is interpreted individually. The attention given the Day of the Lord was transferred to the Lord's Day for Evangelical Friends. For Liberals, the sacramental nature of every day has been secularised: now a day is just any day, religiously speaking. Friends in Florida ask employers to grant the time of their Yearly Meeting as a religious holiday to their Quaker employees. In this example, Friends blend tradition and pragmatism.

Liberal-Liberal Friends do not remember through reference to the endtime. In the figure outlining a biblical sense of time in Chapter 4 (Figure 4.2), twenty-first-century Liberal Friends are off the chart. That whole framework of understanding is alien to most, and for those without a sense of the First Coming, there is equally no Second Coming. Time becomes redundant as a theological motif. There is nothing to remember in John Luffe's sense (see Chapter 2), but also no major global transformation to anticipate, at least none beyond the present-day efforts of humanity. It is thus straightforward to maintain a critical attitude to Christian liturgy with its emphasis on remembrance and anticipation whilst at the same time relinquishing the meta-temporal understanding of early Quaker worship and its concomitant intimacy. Today, Liberal Friends can choose their Gods and choose their intimacies. For Punshon, this is a concern:

> ... outside the Conservative yearly meetings, the unprogrammed meeting is unbalanced. Without words, music or any other formal way of anchoring the worship in the Christian revelation there is no obstacle to the entry of ideas and concepts that are fundamentally inimical to the faith.
>
> (Punshon, 2001, p. 209)

Fenn characterises a secular society as one which has no transcendent vantage point, through sacred history or ideology, and which cannot claim a set of values and beliefs beyond the individual. Society becomes impotent in its ability to act as a mirror for the self, or to mediate or frame the passage of time. The individual instead needs to become immersed in their own destiny, their own sense of time (Fenn, 2001, pp. 20–21). Today, liberal-Liberal Friends choose their own sense of time as they free themselves from the old Christian one: 'The Church is no longer a powerful religious community in a position to mobilize and to pacify its followers, to heighten expectations and also to inure the participants to a long wait for satisfaction' (Fenn, 2001, p. 97).

Unlike the rest of the Church, Quakerism never set out to wait for a promised end point. Rather, it claimed the end was now. It isn't that it has lost its ability to control the meantime, as it never had that in the first place. Quakerism never originally set out to offer a solution to waiting. The Quietist and Evangelical had to find alternative strategies to negotiate the meantime, strategies partly related to the degrees of intimacy the respective groups claimed between themselves and God. Now that there is nothing to wait for in the minds of most Liberal Friends, no lack in the Quaker tradition is felt. There is no felt need to adopt meantime practices such as outward plain dress or Pastors, as there is no felt meantime, only the here and now. Once Liberal Friends had become Liberal, that is, no longer Evangelical with an explicit sense of meantime, the pressure to reform practice disappeared.

Equally, the silence of 'worship' (from 'worth ship', that held worthy) does not require faith. Its outward absence is all-encompassing. For those who maintain belief in something beyond the material, notions of intimacy have become decoupled from ones of the end of time and are sufficient to rationalise a silent approach to mysticism. Rufus Jones did much to place the idea of group mysticism at the heart of modernist Quakerism (for example, Braithwaite, 1912, Introduction), but his reinterpretation of early Quakerism has itself been reinterpreted into a more individualist approach. Jones' idea of 'inner light' is today frequently taken as meaning an individual divinity.

Silence for these Friends is no longer a logical endtime practice or a pragmatic meantime strategy. Both ideas of endtime and meantime are absent from a Liberal Quakerism set outside that Christian understanding of time. It instead functions as the best approach to the unknown for a group highly wary of words. In an ironic paradox, silence is still the medium and the idealised outcome of the encounter that takes place in the silence. Like Bauman's analysis of the seventeenth-century approach (see Chapter 2), today's Friends are frightened of carnal speech in so far as it demeans or misrepresents the depth of religious experience. The sociological difference is that, within the pluralistic Quaker society, theological speech also carries with it the risk of ostracising or ostracisation. Unlike seventeenth-century Quakerism, the boundaries of Quakerism are no longer clear. What it is to be a Liberal Quaker is defined in terms of orthopraxis, not orthodoxy. Theology is relegated to a personal affair. These Friends are not subordinate to the sacred (Martin, 2002, p. 48) but the social.

Daniele Hervieu-Leger has written about the mutation of memory in faith transmission, and how secularisation is accelerated when the memory of faith narratives disappears (2000). Within the modern Liberal Quaker movement, this has occurred implicitly as more and more members join as adults and where mixed Quaker/non-Quaker households diminish the more traditional household discussion of Quakerism. Instead, actors' own accounts become dominant, interpretation of experience often private. The liturgical experience becomes privatised both within and outwith the Meeting House.

Kimon Howland Sargeant, in his study of the baby-boomer 'Seeker Churches' in the US describes how many of these new churches have moved away from 'ritual' as lacking authenticity and expression. Interestingly, there is also a critique of the outward as these churches 'strive to create exciting, innovative, unpredictable events – the opposite of rituals' (2000, p. 56): ' ... genuine faith is best expressed through direct devotion to God. Formal rituals and liturgies can only obstruct this devotion because they all smack of "dead" traditions' (ibid., p. 71).

Building on the work of Mary Douglas (1973, p. 13), Sargeant argues that such a change in form reflects a change in doctrines. New, less formalised rituals have been constructed in Churches that play down denominational affiliation (2000, p. 59). These new rituals are formed within absence. As with their seventeenth-century namesakes, these Seekers have stripped away the outward. This partly reflects the primacy of the inward experience, but is also to minimise connotations of 'Church' for those attending. Rather than the power of religious experience simply making such outward shows redundant, there is also the desire to create a safe space within a secular world where sceptics might feel comfortable. Architecture that used to reflect the mystery and power of God has been replaced with churches which 'emphasize the reasonableness of God and the this-worldly benefits of knowing a God who is not far from the concerns of Americans' (ibid., p. 62). There is a disdain for creeds and tradition – 'relevance' is given greater priority (ibid., p. 63). Contemporary music is a key part of Seeker Church liturgy, as is drama in some cases. As with traditional Quakerism, the Christian calendar is downplayed but in these cases, public holidays form the foci of the Seeker year. As Sargeant comments, the liturgical calendar has been replaced by the Hallmark one (ibid., p. 70).

The emphasis on subjective experience is reflected in the attitude towards the taking of communion. Rather than see the elements as part of the objective presence of God, the emphasis is on the feeling of taking communion, the way in which God is pleased to be remembered (ibid., p. 72). It becomes about an 'emotional encounter with the divine', a relationship of intimacy. As one Pastor puts it: 'If you make a covenant with the Lord [to take communion] ... I think you're going to sense smiles from Heaven; I think God's going to say "That means a lot to me; your covenant moves me. Thanks for caring enough about me to remember me once a month" ' (ibid.).

Douglas Gwyn has drawn out the similarities between early Friends and the seventeenth-century Seeker legacy they partly inherited and the Seeker phenomenon of the present day, the dialectical movement between 'errantry' and 'standing still' and the Seekers looking for new revelation and those seeking for the restoration of old (2000). In earlier work (Dandelion et al., 1998), Gwyn symbolised these two types of Seeker as B and A, respectively (see Chapter 6). In turn I suggested that liberal-Liberal Quakers were perhaps best characterised as a Seeker C type, where the object of the seeking was less important than the seeking itself. Indeed, this group were content to seek anywhere where they would not run the risk of finding (Dandelion, 2001).

However, whilst the subjective element of seeking is shared with Sergeant's Seeker Church sample, the goal of intimacy with God is problematic for many present-day liberal-Liberal Friends, given their uncertainties about the nature of the divine. For some Friends, notions of God have been replaced by something less definite, or have definitely been replaced by something not God.

Mark Chaves argues that denominations are dual entities composed of a 'religious authority structure' as well as an agency structure. The religious agency structure controls the 'access of individuals to some desired good, where the legitimation of that control includes some supernatural component, however weak' (1993, p. 149). Internal secularisation occurs, argues Chaves, when the religious authority structure's control over the agency and its resources diminishes (ibid., p. 165).

The religious authority structure of Liberal Quakerism is diminishing under its own ambivalence about theology, its increasing inability to know what it could say with any certainty, and its increasing clarity that saying anything with any certainty may actually not be very desirable. Seeker C tendencies have become normative so that any theology is provisional, any sense of truth personal or partial. Theology is a towards or perhaps kind of activity whilst, seemingly paradoxically, this position is held with fervent certainty. I have called this phenomenon one of 'absolute perhaps' (Dandelion, forthcoming). Whilst the detail of the religious enterprise can never be known fully or totally, this view is validated from outside of religious experience, from within rationality itself. Rationally, these Quakers are certain that they can never be fully certain about any of their personal or corporate theological claims.

This certainty about uncertainty is an exclusivist position in relation to other religious groups. It says to any group that feels they have found the truth, that they are wrong, and only escapes undermining itself on this count by saying that all groups will be at least partially wrong within their *religious* language games. What is interesting is that this imperialist view across ecumenical frontiers becomes one of timidity across secular ones. Given that theological truth claims are suspect, mission is undermined and the term 'outreach' used instead. Instead of winning and saving souls, Liberal Friends gently impart information about the Quaker option.

For the Quaker faithful, agency becomes increasingly important as a visible sign of the consequences of experience and of organisation itself, a witness to witness as it were. In lines with Chaves' analysis, it is apparent that this work, carried about by a federal agency in the US (American Friends Service Committee) and by Yearly Meeting organisations in Europe (such as Quaker Peace and Social Witness in Britain) has been less and less legitimated by some supernatural component. In this way, *visible* Quakerism, in terms of both outreach and witness, has secularised. Worldly management practices, such as excluding recent Quaker employees from serving on central committees, militates against traditional theological insights. In this example, the employment history of a Quaker serving on a committee, that is, the personal history of any individual on that body, would be irrelevant given the corporate discipline of discernment in which individual will is subsumed to that of the Divine. Has Meeting itself become an agency, separated from a religious authority structure?

Messenger understands that the outward at least offers a visible symbol of that which needs to be remembered (1999, p. 131). For Liberal Friends, their absence of the religiously outward and their disinclination to invent it, may be either attractive as authentic in its sectarian distinctiveness or a pathway to collective amnesia.

At the same time, paradoxically, a few Meetings are arranging regular 'all-age' semi-programmed worship, perhaps even monthly, alongside or instead of the regular unprogrammed event. Typically, a theme is suggested and people come prepared with songs and poems and readings and share as led. The children remain in the Meeting. In Sargeant's terms, this increased outward ritualisation may be a counter to internal secularisation. However, these Meetings are no more necessarily explicitly religious than their unprogrammed counterparts and the driving motivation is inclusivity rather than spiritual hunger. Whilst leadership remains paralysed by fear of disrupting the flat ecclesiology of Quakerism and largely untrained, any amount of programming may only reflect the lowest common denominator of acceptable theological content.

Instead of quaking as itself part of visible revelation, as per Tarter's account of early Friends (see Chapter 3), quaking is absent and silence is now the preparation for the possibility of revelation. Such an open ritual form circumvents the problems of liturgy decontextualising scriptural text in its selective use, of opening Scripture up to multiple readings (see Power, 2001), but silence can decontextualise intent, and open worship up to multiple activities.

In 1989, 692 British Quakers answered the question, 'what kind of activity best describes what are you doing in Meeting for Worship?' as outlined in Figure 7.1.

Praying	34.9
Praising	13.3
Meditating	41.7
Listening	53.8
Communing	29.7
Seeking God's Will	34.3
Seeking Union with the Divine	20.3
Sleeping	6.9
Worshipping God	17.1
Thinking	65.7
Opening Up to the Spirit	60.5

Figure 7.1 British Quaker activity during worship (Dandelion, P., 1996, p. 111)

Given that respondents could tick more than one box, each item becomes a single question. Thus, one in two respondents best classify their worship activity as 'listening', whilst at the same time, two out of three claim that 'thinking' best describes what they do in the silence.

Quaker worship follows a familiar form, and ministry can follow predictable patterns. As well as there being an 'identi-kit' ministry (see Chapter 6), there is an identi-kit meeting. The opening ministry can set the theme for the meeting and whilst subsequent ministries may be thematic, non-thematic, reactive, or even disruptive, a pattern of multiple and mixed-type ministry is typically followed by a 'closing' ministry which attempts to end worship in a positive and constructive manner (Dandelion, P., 1996, pp. 112–18).

However, such predictability, particularly within such an undemanding frame, and within one in which non-speech is so highly prized, means that 'nothing' could pass as a 'gathered' meeting. Doing nothing could pass as spiritual intent. And spiritual intent can be undermined by the infinite imaginations that become possible in the absence of other stimuli. Silence is plain but is also a risky liturgical form. The Quaker rite can be preserved even when feigned:

> Worship is an art and there is a technique which needs to be mastered. Friends have dispensed with the liturgical aids which the vast majority of Christians feel to be necessary, but that does not mean that they are free to ignore all mental disciplines of silent prayer. Otherwise our worship will be nothing more than an unspoken exercise in the psychological game of free association – a succession of day dreams with a religious flavour. A silent meeting can have an air of outward sanctity, and yet be nothing more than a collection of inward chatterings.
>
> (Green, 1983, pp. 13–14)

What happens to transformation?

> ... during all such [spiritual] rituals, the social order is temporarily suspended as individuals move from one status to another. While converts are being transformed from sinner to saved, they are neither in their previous state nor the state they will ultimately attain. Their temporary existence in this ambiguous alternative social structure is determined by the ritual action itself.
>
> (Messenger, 1999, p. 86)

Messenger's view may be overidealistic in some Liberal Quaker settings.

Richard Fenn has developed a typology of ritual requirement for different types of groups, depending on their level of internal integration and their level of separation/distinctiveness from the world (1997, p. 29). In other words, he has charted the kinds of rituals different societies require in order to help them maintain a sense of purpose and most importantly a sense of still having time, that is, not running out of time.

By 'internal integration', Fenn is referring to the 'degree to which personal experience is contained within the framework of prescribed or permitted social interaction, and the degree to which such interaction expresses and reinforces the way the social order assigns duties and accords privileges to its members'. The level of separation from the world Fenn talks of is in relation to how strong the organisational boundaries are between itself and the outside world (ibid., p. 30). Across these two axes, Fenn posits four types of ritual in terms of their primary function: transformation, aversion, purification, and restoration. In these four ways, societies, explicitly religious or otherwise, 'buy' time and maintain cohesion and integration. His typology, and the explanation of these types of ritual, are illustrated in Figure 7.2.

For early Friends, with high internal integration and high levels of separation from the world, rituals of transformation would be required in order to provide an adequate 'temporal matrix' (ibid., p. 30) for the maintenance of the organisation. Rituals of transformation create new chapters of time and renew the social order (ibid., p. 41). Fenn's analysis fits with the discussion in Chapters 1 and 2 about the

The degree of internal integration	The degree to which a social system is differentiated from nature and from other societies	
	High	Low
High	1. TRANSFORMATION	2. AVERSION
Low	3. PURIFICATION	4. RESTORATION

Type of ritual	The manufacture of time
1. Transformation	Creation of a new chapter in the life of the individual, e.g. through initiation into adulthood, marriage or the ancestral community; *the renewal of the social order over time.*
2. Aversion	Reinforcing the integration of self with the conventions of social interaction and the constraints of social organization; *buying time for the social system.*
3. Purification	Separating the present from the past by resolving grievances and expelling outside influences from the community; *the renewal of 'the times'.*
4. Restoration	The recreation of a period of original vigour and harmony in the life of the society; initiating a future that is a sharp break from the present; the restoration of a mythic past.

Figure 7.2 Types of ritual and the manufacture of time (Fenn, 1997, p. 41)

early Quaker liturgical understanding of time and intimacy, how they acted as frameworks for an alternate social and theological ordering, and how such frameworks acted as a guarantee of a particular future (ibid., p. 65).

Quietists maintained this form of ritual, seeking to create separated time and lives away from 'the natural'. They looked to be transformed out of this world, of the everyday sense of time, into their own (see Chapter 3 above).

The Evangelical Friends of the nineteenth century and the modernist ones of the twentieth century lowered the boundaries to the outside world whilst maintaining high levels of internal integration (see Chapter 4 above). It could be argued that the organisation instituted an understanding of ritual as purification, marking a clear break with the Quietist and Hicksite Quaker traditions, expelling and disowning such contamination, and making a clear new start. Holiness experience could nail every vile affection to the cross, and allowed the perfected life to be lived (Hamm, 1988, p. 78). Liberal modernists, with their sense of religion as progress continued this trajectory in a different way 'the nonconformists of the nonconformists' and along with Empire, the civilising influence in the world (Phillips, 1989, p. 33).

For those groups with low internal integration but still a high degree of separation from the world, the case of liberal-Liberal Friends in terms of their religious enterprise if not their life outside of Meeting, we would expect 'rituals of aversion'. These rituals avert disaster and 'buy more time' (Fenn, 1997, p. 41) and 'preserve unity between personal experience, interaction and the social order: to keep people in formation even when their deepest emotions are engaged' (ibid., p. 49). Thus it is within the minimalist but explicit management of silence in the present-day Liberal Quaker liturgical context. Basically, the group is held back from fragmentation at an outward level by the explicit ritual of inward aversion, away from the outward in terms of belief statements and the worldly in terms of form.

If there is a shift here, it will be towards a Quakerism with low levels of separation from the world and low levels of internal integration. In these societies, people can pick and choose their values, ideas, allegiances and the location of use of their economic and social capital (ibid., p. 57). As the liberal-Liberal form of Quakerism becomes increasingly optional in terms of testimony and even attendance, the function of ritual may move to one of 'restoration'. As Fenn argues: 'The hope for restoration comes ... when there is no other hope for preventing a society run out of time' (ibid., p. 151), that is, when ideas of transformation, purification and aversion have lost their currency and efficacy. In a sense, the early Seekers, particularly Type A, were in this mode. They had stripped away the apostate forms and were waiting for the restoration of primitive Christianity. Only when George Fox arrived did those who joined him feel they had the means to transformation looking back to a harmonious vision of a mythic past. What is interesting about restoration in a liberal-Liberal context, is that it needs to balance historic religious and secular sensibilities.

Gay Pilgrim suggests that liberal-Liberal Quakerism in Britain has divided into three types of participant: exclusivists, who have left (such as the Conservative Friends in Christ); inclusivists, who are content to worship within the traditional corporate ecclesiology, and syncretists, who follow their own personal journey without concern for the corporate structures (Pilgrim, 2004). The sense of difference or otherness which Friends have so long cultivated has been turned within the group as the dissonance between Quakerism and the world dwindles so forcefully: if Quakers cannot be different from the world, that impulse means that they now seek to be different from each other. Another way of describing the inclusivists would be as corporatists, with those no longer participating in the corporate structures as locally-focused congregationalists, or individualists (Dandelion, B.P., 1996).

Those who are less sectarian and more world-affirming and indeed worldly, may be precipitating a Quaker ritualisation of restoration. In Fenn's terms, restoration is about the attempt to recreate initial vigour and harmony, to restore a mythic past. We might see this in terms of attempts to maintain Quaker insights wrapped in a new theology, or to maintain Quaker form with reference to the early days whilst allowing the basis of form to shift. It is a rearguard action by the corporatists to sustain some coherence and salience in traditional ways. I have argued that the 1995 British *Quaker Faith and Practice* is a classic example of this kind of radical conservatism, seeking to restore God to the Quaker framework albeit at the expense of explicit Christianity (Dandelion, B.P., 1996).

So, we may already be witnessing a dualism of ritual within the liberal-Liberal tradition; indeed it may play out along the lines of the Quaker double culture, the organisation seeking restoration in terms of the liberal belief culture and aversion in terms of maintaining the behavioural creed. If form starts to fragment, then we might expect rituals of restoration to come into play in terms of recreating a mythic past centred on the style of worship. As Quaker business method is questioned by new theology (Redfern, 1993), we can perhaps see the attempts to transmit 'right ordering' through educational videos and workshops within this framework.

In short, whilst the worship of Friends three centuries apart looks the same, it is not. The base understandings of the liturgical form are radically different in terms of both how they relate to endtime and how they relate to intimacy. Second, using Fenn's analysis, the liturgies are functioning to express very different organisational priorities. The seventeenth-century Quaker worship is about transformation, the nineteenth about purification, the twenty-first about aversion and restoration in the face of increasingly low internal integration and low levels of separation between participants and the world.

Fenn argues that ritual offers a way back into magic. When it fails, he suggests, charisma, the personal means to magic, becomes attractive (1997, p. 16). This is not so immediately obvious even within a secularised Quakerism. However, looking more closely, we can see that the charisma that becomes attractive is not that of an authoritarian leader as in Fenn's theory, but of the silence itself. If the silence fails to provide the magic, the silence itself can become revered, for its salve and its potential is enormous even on a secular level. One Friend reported to me that Meeting may only 'work' one time in one hundred, but its potential remains compelling even without the magic. For agnostics and atheists, the silence is safe, the magic never force-fed. Ultimate weight is not given then to a person in liberal-Liberal Quakerism but to the charismatic means to far greater magic. If silence is revered and given authority and policed with such vigour, we can see the clue as to why here. As the social integration of the group diminishes, silence and the aversive ritual it provides becomes even more crucial to the sustenance of itself and the magic it may also provide. Silence thus operates on these two levels, one of buying time, one of buying magic. At a totally secular level, it buys the time and magic of rest in a busy world.

The liberal-Liberal Quakers have lost their sense of working in God's time, and certainly of a biblical understanding of endtime. They have maintained ideas of intimacy. This shift in itself carries with it a diminishment of consequence. There are no liturgical rites to negotiate once all sense of time is out of the picture. Whichever side of the 'Till He Come' you are becomes a non-question, an anachronism. In this sense, liberal-Liberal Friends have moved out of that time of worrying about time. They are out of time, and every day is indeed the same. However, they are out of time in a very different way from the early Friends who saw the day of the Lord unfolding around them. These Friends are out of that time because that time no longer exists for them. The 'Now' is all. Every day is equivalent rather than special. Different approaches to the outward or inward sacraments become equivalent as the arguments for or against lose their meaning. Everyone and everything becomes potentially equivalent and everything becomes optional, Christmas, Easter, Pentecost. Time moves outside of the control of the Church, the feature of secularisation Fenn points out, and people create their own time within their supermarket spiritualities or secularities. People are liberated from control, and from a God who never gave them enough time. Now, people only need to face the 'terrible underside of human freedom' (Dandelion et al., 1998, p. 126) rather than the frightening prospect of obedience to God. God is made plausible, humanised, levelled to the state of human potential (Dandelion et al., 2004, Chapter Five). When the times are good, and for most liberal-Liberal Friends they live in an age and space of so much outward wealth, this can only feel liberating. And they still have intimacy, running to their own time and tune.

Intimacy as an organisational principle is far more relaxed, far less specific and pre-ordered. It looks as if it can be more enduring in a post-Christian age of, say, British Quakerism and more inclusive than specifically Christian doctrine, but also with the potential for greater internal secularisation.

Time and endtime set up exclusivities of people and place and prescribed potential. It was all laid out by Scripture. The Kingdom of God was prefigured in God's plan for the world. It was a specific plan, and every action could take you towards it or away from it. It was also couched in ideas which a rational faith found difficult to sustain and embarrassing to maintain in the face of a growing ecumenical temperament. When Quakerism ceased to be the true Church in the 1830s, it was first of all part of the true Church. Now the whole of people of God can take their pick of any one or none of a number of ways up the mountain, or around it, or down. Quakers can be dual-members with churches with historically opposite understandings of worship because silent worship can now be reduced to silence, an empty form which can include so much, or nothing.

And for some the mountain of the kingdom isn't a mountain. The liberalisation of post-millennialism becomes simply secular, a time ahead to aim for with the best intentions. As Bryan Wilson has said of present-day Quakers, they are a 'reformist sect', that is, they seek 'salvation' by trying to reform conscience (1970, p. 38). Now humanity can simply take its separate paths towards an undefined horizon which can be imagined along the way.

Ultimately, then, the present-day liberal-Liberal intimacy need no longer be God-centric. It can be far less rationally awkward, and far more inclusive, given the diversity of believing within the group. The worship method need not change, only its basis. British Quakers still mention God in their descriptions of worship (see Chapter 5) and the book of discipline, composed and agreed by the corporatists, still suggests that God, if not Christ, is part of the Quaker equation of worship. But such truth is now personal, partial, or provisional, and no one can or would want to enforce such understandings on the Quaker in the street. That is why the specific theology is so absent and the silence so prized.

For some, the intimacy is no longer with God but with self and with community. Far removed from Quietistic ideas of the annihilation of self, psychological insights have been incorporated into the liberal-Liberal kaleidoscope of believing. The self is important, to be nurtured, and even praised. Divinity resides there in versions of Jonesian and (Matthew) Foxian cosmologies. For these Friends, the intimacy is no longer inward but inner. As time has become personalised, no longer running to someone's else's (for example, God's) timetable, so has intimacy. Meeting becomes a private affair, individualised on chairs instead of benches. Ministry comes from the heart or the head but from the person, not God. Quakers thank each other for their ministry not each other for being faithful vessels. Thinking is the most popular activity in Meeting, not dying to the self. Instead of Gurney's sense that silent worship was the best vehicle for a humiliation of self before God (see Chapter 4), the self can be placed at the centre of a privatised quiet.

The history of Quakerism becomes a useful resource to justify practice but not to enforce it. All our discussion here of Fox, Barclay and Gurney is irrelevant to most liberal-Liberal Quakers and is certainly not central to their discussion of worship. Where there is an 'intimacy' with Quaker history, this itself limits the potential for the profane with its emphasis on historical time and its historicisation of the spiritual. Jones and Rowntree, believing history could unlock revival, may have instead constrained it with their emphasis on the historical past.

Having the table in or out of the centre is about a personal preference rather than a theological position. If the table bedecked with flowers is a quasi-altar, it is in celebration of an aesthetic. Right or wrong, the point here is that the liberal-Liberal understanding of worship is of another sort to the rest of Quakerism whose understandings can be more or less traced to earlier Quaker insights. Silent worship is not necessarily the same as silent worship.

There may be no experience left to feign, other than the self-made one. As Flanagan states, 'silence carries a penetrating and inescapable element of ambiguity' (1991, p. 251), both presence and absence and all the emotions both can give rise to. Otto wrote of silent waiting as 'a preparation of the soul to become the pencil of the unearthly writer' (1923, p. 217). Silence can be the beginning and the end of authentic religious expression. At the same time, where God does not exist for those present, the absence is absolute. Silent worship then is no longer a consequence of a keen sense of the inward covenant of Jeremiah 31 or a means to the inward supper of Revelation 3:20 but is an end in itself. Liberal-Liberal worship holds both these possibilities in tension at present. The worship is generally not understood in traditionally Quaker ways even whilst some are still enagaged in a personal relationship with a God who gathers and guides. It is seen as a method equivalent to other church forms and the theological underpinning marginal compared with the experience possible in the silence. The danger of this shift away from theological specificity is that it allows other and even secular interpretations to become part of the normative Quaker fabric within this tradition. This kind of Quakerism, now always in transition, remains worthy of continuing theological and sociological attention. In each decade, it will be possible to ask, 'and what kind of liturgy (or "liturgy"?) are these Quakers operating now?' It is a flexibility that may even allow for the success of restorationist ritual, and a move amongst liberal-Liberal Friends to return to a more distinctively traditional Quaker understanding of the nature of their practice. We will see.

Bibliography

Allen, R. (1992), *Silence and Speech*, London: Quaker Home Service.

Anderson, P. (n.d), 'Meet the Friends: Friends and worship', Newberg, OR: Department of Christian Testimonies, Northwest Yearly Meeting of Friends Church.

Baer, R.A. (1975), 'Silent Worship, Glossolalia and Liturgy: some functional similarities', *Quaker Religious Thought*, **16** (3), pp. 28–37.

Bailey, R. (1992), *New Light on George Fox and Early Quakerism: the making and unmaking of a God*, San Francisco, CA. Mellen Research University Press.

Bailey, R. (2004), 'Was Seventeenth Century Quaker Christology Homogeneous?', in Dandelion, P. (ed.), *The Creation of Quaker Theory: insider perspectives*, Aldershot: Ashgate, pp. 61–82.

Baptism, Eucharist and Ministry (1982) (Faith and Order Paper No. 111), Geneva: World Council of Churches.

Barbour, H. and Roberts, A.O. (1973), *Early Quaker Writings 1650–1700*, Grand Rapids, MI: Eerdmans.

Barclay, R. (2002) [1678], *Apology for the True Christian Divinity*, Glenside, PA: Quaker Heritage Press.

Bauman, R. (1974) 'Speaking in the Light: the role of the Quaker minister', in Bauman, R. and Sherzer, J. (eds), *Explorations in the Ethnography of Speaking*, Cambridge: Cambridge University Press, pp. 144–60.

Bauman, R. (1983), *Let Your Words be Few: symbolism of speaking and silence amongst seventeenth-century Quakers*, Cambridge: Cambridge University Press.

Bell, D. (1977), 'Stranger in the Meeting', *The Friend*, **135**, pp. 5–6.

Binns, J. (2002), *An Introduction to the Christian Orthodox Churches*, Cambridge: Cambridge University Press.

Book of Extracts (1783), London: London Yearly Meeting.

Blackborrow, S. (1663), 'To the Reader', in *A Collection of the Several Books and Writings of that Faithful Servant of God Richard Hubberthorne*, London.

Braithwaite, W.C. (1912), *The Beginnings of Quakerism*, London: Macmillan.

Braithwaite, W.C. (1919), *The Second Period of Quakerism*, London: Macmillan.

Bria, I. (1996), *The Liturgy After the Liturgy: mission and witness from an Orthodox perspective*, Geneva: World Council of Churches Publications.

Brinton, H.H. (2002), *Friends for 350 years*, revised edn, Wallingford, PA: Pendle Hill.

Britain Yearly Meeting Proceedings (1997) London: Britain Yearly Meeting.

Britten, W. (1660), *Silent meeting … a wonder to the world*, London.

Brown, D. and Loades, A. (eds) (1995), *The Sense of the Sacramental: movement and measure in art and music, place and time*, London: SPCK.

Burrough, E. (1656), *The Trumpet of the Lord Sounded Forth Out of Zion*, London.

Burrough, E. (1657), *A Standard Lifted Up*, London: Giles Calvert.

Burrough, E. (1672), *Memorable Works of a Son of Thunder*. No publication details available.

Carrdus, A. (1993), 'The Quaker Unchristmas', *The Friend*, **151**, pp. 1659–60.

Chauvet, L.-M. (1995), *Symbol and Sacrament: a sacramental reinterpretation of Christian existence*, trans. Madigan, P. and Beaumont, M., Collegeville, MN: Pueblo Books.

Chaves, M. (1993), 'Denominations as Dual Structures: an organizational analysis', *Sociology of Religion*, **54**, pp. 147–69.

Child, J. (1995), 'Down There is Where I Need to Be', in Duke, E. (ed.), *Readings on Worship*, London: Quaker Home Service, pp. 11–13.

Coleman, S. and Collins, P. (2000) 'The "Plain" and the "Positive": ritual, experience and aesthetics in Quakerism and charismatic Christianity', *Journal of Contemporary Religion*, **15**, pp. 317–29.

Collinge-Hill, E. (2001), 'The Experience of Worship: a study of worship in England at the millennium', unpublished M.Phil. thesis, University of Birmingham.

Collins, P.J. (1996), ' "Plaining": the social and cognitive practice of symbolisation in the Religious Society of Friends (Quakers)', *Journal of Contemporary Religion*, **11**, pp. 277–88.

Collins, P.J. and Dandelion, P. (2001), 'Wrapped Attention: revelation and concealment in non-conformism', Paper presented at the British Sociological Association Sociology of Religion Study Group Annual Conference, Plater College, Oxford.

Common Worship, Services and Prayers for the Church of England (2002), London: Church House Publishing.

Cope, W. (ed.) (2001), *Heaven on Earth: 101 happy poems*, London: Faber and Faber.

Cowie, I. (1990), 'On Not Having a Creed', *The Staffordshire Quaker*, September, p. 7.

Creasey, M.A. (1962) ' "Inward" and "Outward": a study in early Quaker language', Supplement No. 30, *Journal of the Friends Historical Society*, pp. 1–24.

Crisp, S. (1707), *Scripture Truths Demonstrated: in thirty-two sermons or declarations of Mr Stephen Crisp, late of Colchester in Essex, deceased* ..., London: J. Sowle.

Crumbine, N.J. (1975), 'On Silence', *Humanitas*, May, pp. 147–65.

Dalmais, I.H. (1987), 'The Liturgy as Celebration of the Mystery of Salvation', in Martimort, A.G. (ed.), *The Church at Prayer*, vol. 1, 'Principles of Liturgy', trans. O'Connell, M.J., London: Geoffrey Chapman, pp. 253–72.

Damiano, K. (1988), 'On Earth as it is in Heaven: eighteenth century Quakerism as realized eschatology', unpublished Ph.D. thesis, Union of Experimenting Colleges and Universities.

Dandelion, B.P. (1996) 'From Lymbo to Bymbo', *Friends Quarterly*, **28**, pp. 163–70.

Dandelion, B.P., Gwyn, D. and Peat, T. (1998), *Heaven on Earth: Quakers and the second coming*, Birmingham and Kelso: Woodbrooke and Curlew.

Dandelion, P. (1996), *A Sociological Analysis of the Theology of Quakers: the silent Revolution*, Lampeter: Edwin Mellen Press.

Dandelion, P. (2001), 'From Religion to Ethics: Quaker amillennialism', in Flanagan, K. and Jupp, P. (eds), *Virtue Ethics and Sociology: issues of modernity and religion*, Basingstoke: Palgrave, pp. 170–85.

Dandelion, P. (2002), 'Those Who Leave and Those Who Feel Left: the complexity of Quaker disaffiliation', *Journal of Contemporary Religion*, **17**, pp. 213–28.

Dandelion, P. (forthcoming), 'Implicit Conservatism in Liberal Religion: British Quakers as an 'uncertain sect', *Journal of Contemporary Religion*.

Dandelion, P., Gwyn, D., Muers, R., Phillips, B. and Sturm, R.E. (2004), *Towards Tragedy/ Reclaiming Hope*, Aldershot: Ashgate.

Davie, G. (1994), *Religion in Britain Since 1945: believing without belonging*, Oxford: Blackwell.

Davies, A. (1988), 'Talking in Silence: Ministry in Quaker Meetings', in Coupland, N. (ed.), *Styles of Discourse*, London: Croom Helm, pp. 105–37.

Davies, D. (2002), *Anthropology and Theology*, Oxford: Berg.

'Declaration of Faith as Issued by the Richmond Conference', (1887), in *The Faith and Practice of Friends Church Southwest Yearly Meeting* (1987), Whittier, CA: Friends Church Southwest Yearly Meeting, pp. 10–25.

Dewsbury, W. (1689), *A Faithful Testimony of that Ancient Servant of the Lord*, London.

A Distinction Between the Two Suppers (1991), Gloucester: George Fox Fund.

Dix, G. (1946), *The Shape of the Liturgy*, London: Dacre Press.

Doherty, R.W. (1967), *The Hicksite Separation: a sociological analysis of religious schism in early nineteenth-century America*, New Brunswick, NJ: Rutgers University Press.

Douglas, M. (1973), *Natural Symbols*, New York: Pantheon.

Dunn, J.D.G. (1991), *The Parting of the Ways: between Christianity and Judaism and their significance for the character of Christianity*, London: SCM Press.

Ellwood, T. (1885), *The History of Thomas Ellwood by Himself*, London: George Routledge.

Faith and Practice: a book of Christian discipline, Northwest Yearly Meeting of Friends Church (1998), Newberg, OR: Northwest Yearly Meeting.

Faith and Practice – Book of Discipline of the North Carolina Yearly Meeting (Conservative) of the Religious Society of Friends (1983), Ahoskie, NC: Pierce Printing.

The Faith and Practice of Friends Church Southwest Yearly Meeting (1987), Whittier, CA: Friends Church Southwest Yearly Meeting.

Farnsworth, R. (1663), *The Spirit of God Speaking in the Temple of God*, London.

Fenn, R.K. (1995), *The Persistence of Purgatory*, Cambridge: Cambridge University Press.

Fenn, R.K. (1997), *The End of Time: religion, ritual, and the forging of the soul*, London: SPCK.

Fenn, R.K. (2001), *Time Exposure: the personal experience of time in secular societies*, Oxford: Oxford University Press.

Flanagan, K. (1991), *Sociology and Liturgy: re-presentations of the holy*, London: Macmillan.

Flannery, A. (ed.) (1975), *Vatican council II: the conciliar and post-conciliar documents*, Dublin: Dominican Publications.

Fox, G. (1659), *The Great Mistery of the Great Whore Unfolded*, London.

Fox, G. (1891), *The Journal of George Fox*, Bicentenary edition, 2 vols, London: Friends Tract Association.

Fox, G. (1911), *The Journal of George Fox*, ed. Penney, N., vol. 1, London: Cambridge University Press.

Fox, G. (1952), *The Journal of George Fox*, ed. Nickalls, J., Cambridge: Cambridge University Press.

Fox, G. (1990), *Works*, 8 vols, State College, PA: New Foundation Publications.

Freiday, D. (1967), *Barclay's Apology in Modern English*, New Jersey: privately published.

Frost, W.J. (1973), *The Quaker Family in Colonial America*, New York: St Martin's Press.

Giles, H. and Powesland, P.F. (1975), *Speech Style and Social Evaluation*, London: Academic Press.

Graves, M.P. (1972), 'The Rhetoric of the Inward Light: an examination of extant sermons delivered by early Quakers, 1671–1700', unpublished Ph.D. thesis, University of Southern California.

Green, D.A. (1978), 'The Era of Transition, 1750–1840', in Hall, F.B. (ed.), *Quaker Worship in North America*, Richmond, IN: Friends United Press, pp. 37–52.

Green, T. (1983), *Preparation for Worship* (Swarthmore Lecture, 1952), London: Quaker Home Service.

Gurney, J.J. (1979 [transcript of *Observations on the Distinguishing Views and Practices of the Society of Friends*, seventh edn, 1834], *A Peculiar People: the rediscovery of primitive Christianity*, Richmond, IN: Friends United Press.

Gwyn, D. (1981), ' "Into That Which Cannot be Shaken": the apocalyptic Gospel preached by George Fox', in Freiday, D. (ed.), *The Day of the Lord: eschatology in Quaker perspective*, Newberg, OR: Barclay Press, pp. 61–96.

Gwyn, D. (1986), *Apocalypse of the Word: the life and message of George Fox, 1624–1691*, Richmond, IN: Friends United Press.

Gwyn, D. (1995), *Covenant Crucified: Quakers and the rise of capitalism*, Wallingford, PA: Pendle Hill.

Gwyn, D. (2000), *Seekers Found: atonement in early Quaker experience*, Wallingford, PA: Pendle Hill.

Hahn, S. (2003), *The Lamb's Supper: the Mass as heaven on earth*, London: Dartman, Longman and Todd.

Hamm, T.D. (1988), *The Transformation of American Quakerism: Orthodox Friends 1800–1907*, Bloomington, IN: Indiana University Press.

Heilman, S.C. (1976), *Synagogue Life*, Chicago: University of Chicago Press.

Hendry, J. (1993), *Wrapping Culture: politeness, presentation and power in Japan and other societies*, Oxford: Clarendon Press.

Heron, A. (1992), *Caring, Conviction, Commitment: dilemmas of Quaker membership today*, London: Quaker Home Service.

Hervieu-Leger, D. (2000), *Religion as a Chain of Memory*, trans. S. Lee, Oxford: Polity Press.

Hewitt, J. (1990), 'Embracing Uncertainty', *The Friend*, **148**, pp. 757–58.

Homan, R. (2000), 'The Art of Joseph Edward Southall', *Quaker Studies*, 5, pp. 69–83.

Homan, R. (2001), 'Engaging in Worship', *New Directions*, December, pp. 12–23.

Hubbard, G. (1992), *Quaker by Convincment*, revised edn, London: Quaker Home Service.

Hughes, G. (1986), *In Search of a Way: two journeys of spiritual discovery*, second edn, London: Dartman, Longman and Todd.

Isichei, E. (1967), 'From Sect to Denomination Among English Quakers', in Wilson, B.R. (ed.), *Patterns of Sectarianism: organisation and ideology in social and religious movements*, London: Heinemann, pp. 161–81.

Isichei, E. (1970), *Victorian Quakers*, Oxford: Oxford University Press.

Jensen, V.V. (1973), 'Communicative Functions of Silence', *ETC*, **30**, pp. 249–57.

Johns, D.L. (1998), 'Ritual Management of Presence and Absence: the liturgical significance of silence', *Quaker Religious Thought*, **28** (4), pp. 31–42.

Jones, R.M. (1921), *The Later Periods of Quakerism*, 2 vols, London: Macmillan.

Kaiser, G. (1994), *The Society of Friends in North America*, Chart, 17th edn, Sumneytown, PA: privately published.

Kelly, T. (1944), *The Gathered Meeting*, London: Friends Home Service Committee.

Kennedy, T.C. (2001), *British Quakerism 1860–1920: The transformation of a religious community*, Oxford: Oxford University Press.

Kirk. J. (1978), 'Worship that comes from Programming in the United Meeting Tradition', in Hall, F.B. (ed.), *Quaker Worship in North America*, Richmond, IN: Friends United Press, pp. 87–104.

Leichty, D. (1990), *Theology in Postliberal Perspective*, London: SCM.

Lippard, P.V. (1988), 'The Rhetoric of Silence: the Society of Friends Unprogrammed Meeting for Worship', *Communication Quarterly*, **36** (2), pp. 145–56.

Loughlin, G. (2000), 'Time' in Hastings, A., Mason, A. and Pyper, H. (eds), *The Oxford Companion to Christian Thought*, Oxford: Oxford University Press, pp. 707–09.

Mack, P. (1992), *Visionary Women: ecstatic prophecy in seventeenth-century England*, Berkeley: University of California Press.

Maltz, D.N. (1985), 'Joyful Noise and Reverent Silence: the significance of noise in Pentecostal worship', in Tannen, D. and Saville-Troike, M. (eds), *Perspectives on Silence*, Norwood, NJ: Ablex Publishing, pp. 113–37.

Marietta, J.D. (1984), *The Reformation of American Quakerism, 1748–83*, Philadelphia, PA: University of Pennsylvania Press.

Martin, D. (2002), *Christian Language and its Mutations: essays in sociological understanding*, Aldershot: Ashgate.

Messenger, T. (1999), *Holy Leisure: recreation and religion in God's square mile*, Philadelphia, PA: Temple University Press.

Mingins, R. (2003), 'Light Within or Beacon Without? An evaluation of the impact of evangelicalism on Quakers 1820–1840', *Quaker Studies*, **8**, pp. 51–67.

Moore, R. (2001), *The Light in their Consciences: the early Quakers in Britain 1646–1666*, University Park, PA: Pennsylvania State University Press.

Mylander, C. (1978), 'Evangelical Friends Worship', in Hall, F.B. (ed.), *Quaker Worship in North America*, Richmond, IN: Friends United Press, pp. 123–40.

Nickalls, J. (ed.) (1952), *The Journal of George Fox*, Cambridge: Cambridge University Press.

Nuhn, F. (1981), 'The Peaceable Kingdom: the Quaker witness and the Judeo-Christian hope', in Freiday, D. (ed.), *The Day of the Lord: eschatology in Quaker perspective*, Newberg, OR: Barclay Press, pp. 30–40.

O'Shea, U.J. (1993), *Living the Way: Quaker spirituality and community*, The Religious Society of Friends (Quakers) in Australia Incorporated.

Otto, R. (1923), *The Idea of the Holy: an inquiry in the non-rational factor of the idea of the divine and its relation to the rational*, trans. J.W. Harvey, Oxford: Oxford University Press.

Penington, I. (1996), *The Works of Isaac Penington: a minister of the gospel in the Society of Friends*. Vol. III., Glenside, PA: Quaker Heritage Press.

Phillips, B.D. (1989), 'Friendly Patriotism: British Quakerism and the imperial nation, 1890–1910', unpublished Ph.D. thesis, University of Cambridge.

Pickvance, J. (1989), *A Reader's Companion to George Fox's Journal*, London: Quaker Home Service.

Pilgrim, G. (2004), 'Taming Anarchy: Quaker alternate ordering and "otherness"', in Dandelion, P. (ed.), *The Creation of Quaker Theory: insider perspectives*, Aldershot: Ashgate, pp. 206–25.

Power, D.N. (2001), *'The Word of the Lord': liturgy's use of scripture*, Maryknoll, NY: Orbis.

Punshon, J. (1987), *Encounter with Silence: reflections from the Quaker tradition*, Richmond, IN and London: Friends United Press and Quaker Home Service.

Punshon, J. (1989), *Letter to a Universalist*, Pendle Hill Pamphlet No. 285, Wallingford, PA: Pendle Hill.

Punshon, J. (2001), *Reasons for Hope: the faith and future of the Friends Church*, Richmond, IN: Friends United Press.

Quaker Faith and Practice: the book of Christian discipline in the Yearly Meeting of the Religious Society of Friends (Quakers) in Britain (1995), London: Britain Yearly Meeting.

'The Quaker Way' (1998), London: Quaker Home Service, pamphlet.

'Quaker Worship' (1989), London: Britain Yearly Meeting, pamphlet.

Rahner, K. (1975), *Encyclopedia of Theology: a concise sacramentum mundi*, London: Burns and Oates.

Redfern, K. (1993), *What are our Monthly Meetings Doing? A concern for the revitalization of meetings for business, 1992–1993*, London: Quaker Home Service.

Reynolds, G. (2004), 'Was George Fox a Gnostic?', unpublished Ph.D. thesis, University of Sunderland.

The Roman Missal (1975) Alcester and Dublin: C. Goodliffe Neal.

Rosenberg, B.A. (1970) 'The Formulaic Quality of Spontaneous Sermons', *Journal of American Folklore*, 83, pp. 3–20.

Samarin, W.J. (1965), 'Language of Silence', *Practical Anthropology*, **12**, pp. 115–19.

Sargeant, K.H. (2000), *Seeker Churches; promoting traditional religion in a nontraditional way*, New Brunswick, NJ: Rutgers University Press.

Schweitzer, A. (1968), *The Quest for the Historical Jesus*, New York: Macmillan.

Scott, J. (1980), *What Canst Thou Say? Towards a Quaker Theology*, London: Quaker Home Service.

Shils, E. (1965), 'Charisma, Order, and Status', *American Sociological Review*, **30**, pp. 199–213.

Siler, E.C. (1887), 'The Pastoral Question', *Christian Worker*, **17**, pp. 397–401.

Somerville, J. (1992), *The Secularization of Early Modern England: from religions culture to religious faith*, London: Oxford University Press.

Spencer, C. (2004), 'Holiness: the Quaker way of perfection', in Dandelion, P. (ed.), *The Creation of Quaker Theory: insider perspectives*, Aldershot: Ashgate, pp. 149–71.

Stringer, M. (1999), *On the Perception of Worship: the ethnography of worship in four Christian congregations in Manchester*, Birmingham: University of Birmingham Press.

Taber, W.P. Jr (1978), 'Worship in the Conservative Tradition', in Hall, F.B. (ed.), *Quaker Worship in North America*, Richmond, IN: Friends United Press, pp. 75–86.

Tarter, M.L. (1993), 'Sites of Performance: theorizing the history of sexuality in the lives and writing of Quaker women, 1650–1800', unpublished Ph.D. thesis, University of Colorado.

Tarter, M.L. (2001), 'Quaking in the Light: the politics of Quaker women's corporeal prophecy in the seventeenth-century transatlantic world', in Lindman, J.M., and Tarter, M.L. (eds), *A Centre of Wonders: the body in early America*, Ithaca, NY: Cornell University Press, pp. 145–62.

To Lima with Love. Baptism, Eucharist and Ministry: a Quaker response (1986), London: Quaker Home Service.

Tousley, N.C. (2003), 'The Experience of Regeneration and Erosion of Certainty in the Theology of Second-Generation Quakers: no place for doubt?', unpublished M.Phil. thesis, University of Birmingham.

Tuke, S. (1824), *Memoirs of the Life of Stephen Crisp with Selections from his Works*, York: Alexander and Son.

Vann, R.T. (1969), *The Social Development of English Quakerism, 1655–1755*, Cambridge, MA: Harvard University Press.

Walke, B. (2002), *Twenty Years at St Hilary*, Truro: Truran.

Weick, K.E. (1987), 'Organizational Culture as a Source of High Reliability', *Californian Management Review*, **29** (Winter), pp. 112–27.

Weiss, E. (1987), *City in the Woods: the life and design of an American camp meeting on Martha's Vineyard*, Oxford: Oxford University Press.

'Welcome to our Meeting' (n.d.), Barnesville, OH: Ohio Yearly Meeting.

White, D. (1659), *Friends, you that are of the Parliament, hear the word of the Lord*.

White, S.J. (2000), 'Liturgy' in Hastings, A., Mason, A. and Pyper, H. (eds), *The Oxford Companion to Christian Thought*, Oxford: Oxford University Press, pp. 391–93.

Wilson, B.R. (1970), *Religious Sects*, London: Weidenfield and Nicholson.

Wood, R.E. (1978), 'The Rise of Semi-Structured Worship and Paid Pastoral Leadership among "Gurneyite" Friends, 1850–1900', in Hall, F.B. (ed.), *Quaker Worship in North America*, Richmond, IN: Friends United Press, pp. 53–74.

Woods, J. (2002), 'The Context and Experience of Quaker Worship in the Early Years 1650–1675 with Some Reference to Yorkshire', unpublished M.A. thesis, University of York.
'Yearly Meeting Minutes' (1880), London: London Yearly Meeting.
'Your First Time in Meeting?' (1997), London: Britain Yearly Meeting.
Zielinski, S. (1975), *Psychology and Silence*, Pendle Hill Pamphlet No. 210, Wallingford, PA: Pendle Hill.

Index